CLASSIC ROCK CLIMBS

PAUL DEARDEN

BLANDFORD

A BLANDFORD BOOK
First published in the UK 1994
by Blandford
(a Cassell imprint)
Villiers House
41/47 Strand
LONDON
WC2N 5JE

British Library Cataloguing-in-Publication Data
A catalogue record for this book is available from the British Library

ISBN 0-7137-2436-6

Printed and bound in Great Britain by Mackays of Chatham plc
Typeset by Goodfellow & Egan, Cambridge

Contents

PREFACE   vii

INTRODUCTION   ix

SOUTH WALES   1
Ogmore   1
Gower   5
Pembrokeshire   10
The Valleys   15
Wye Valley   19

WEST COUNTRY   25
Avon   25
Cheddar Gorge   30

DEVON AND CORNWALL   36
Lower Sharpnose
   Point   36
Lundy   40
Carn Gowla and
   Bass Point   45
Dartmoor and
   Torquay   49

SOUTHERN ENGLAND   54
Swanage   54
Jersey   58
Beachy Head   62

PEAK DISTRICT   67
The Burbage Valley   67
Chee Dale   72
Wimberry   76

YORKSHIRE   80

NORTHUMBERLAND   85

LAKE DISTRICT   89
Borrowdale   89
Southern Lakes   93

LANCASHIRE   98

NORTH WALES   103
Clywd   103
Holy Island and
   Llandudno   108
Bank Holiday Climbs   113
Dinorwic Slate   118

INDEX   123

PREFACE

As a teenager I read the autobiographies of people like Brown and Whillans, and came into climbing through an apprenticeship of Lockwood's Chimney, Doorpost in the rain and Little Chamonix in a group of 25 on New Year's Eve. On my sixteenth birthday I climbed Great Slab at Millstone – after the Hathersage Inn had shut! Whatever else I was doing, I was enjoying the adventure, the unpredictability and the sheer fun of it all. Most Friday nights would find us heading off to some unknown area of the country with a few photocopied notes from a guidebook or a magazine, and late on Sunday we would head home exhausted, but happy.

Climbing has become more popular since then, and it has changed in many ways. I have trained, used chalk, spent days on a single route (and still not finished it) and even taken holidays in the sun at Christmas instead of going to North Wales. Many people come into climbing now through indoor walls, and an increasing feature of such walls is the competitions they seem to breed. It is now possible to become a 'good climber' without ever going to the mountains, or even the gritstone edges of Derbyshire. Climbing walls can be fun, yet the times I still enjoy most revolve around climbing in beautiful or unusual places, climbing with good friends – perhaps when things don't go exactly to plan.

The purpose of this book is to describe some of the less popular places where I have found fun, so that people will be encouraged to visit new locations. Climbing in Britain offers such a variety of experience, and I hope to have illustrated something new for most people. I have climbed all but a handful of the routes described, and I have had a go at the others!

Different routes have been memorable to me for different reasons. When it is all over, we are only the sum of our memories. This book is for all those who have helped me make my memories, but especially for Anthony Wright, who first took me into the hills; for Eddie Hutchinson, who gave me all manner of good advice; and for Andy Fanshawe, whose energy was an inspiration to us all.

INTRODUCTION

Rock climbing as a pastime has come a long way since the late eighteenth century, when the early pioneers first set about exploring the cliffs of Britain. Is it possible that the few eccentrics who scrambled up the damp and often dirty gullies that formed many of the early climbs knew that in a hundred years there would be scores of people, of all ages and backgrounds, meeting in old factories of a winter's evening to practise the same art, albeit on drier, cleaner and artificial rock?

The process by which climbing has become an acceptable mass participation sport is an interesting one, and probably an inevitable one too. It is not surprising that activities like bungee jumping seem to be following in the same way, with the commercialization possibilities being realized much more quickly.

In the early days, climbing was as much a spiritual as a physical activity. The place, the company and the natural forces that combined in rock and weather were the prime elements, and the result was distilled into memories as powerful as the experience itself. Climbing has always been a competitive sport – of that there is no doubt – but one in which the competition used to provide motivation rather than reward. Many of the early climbs were audacious undertakings, not because of technical difficulty but because of the unknown dangers that might lie ahead.

Inevitably, the first step forward was one of consolidation in numbers. More people came into climbing with the convenient goal of repeating some of the pioneering achievements before creating new routes themselves. With a growth in documentation, it must have seemed obvious to match your skills against an established yardstick before turning to more adventurous challenges. Very soon, the first guidebooks were produced, with a grading system for difficulties emerging. Once enough people are writing and talking about an activity enthusiastically, its growth is assured. With information becoming available on a second-hand basis in guidebooks, swifter growth followed.

However, the amount of new rock for the pioneers to test themselves on was always going to be limited, and so the next leap forward was the use of artificial aids to enable 'unclimbable' sections of rock to be bypassed. This opened up enormous new areas of steep cliffs and, despite some initial criticism, it was quickly accepted as the norm. With the increased level of protection provided by pitons, the standards achieved rose quickly. Better dissemination led to a more competitive edge, and this again fuelled the rise in standards.

The growth in numbers made climbing a more viable market for commercial initiatives, and the next advances were down to industrial skill as much as anything. Boots, ropes and protection all improved in significant little jumps as the market expanded. Parallel to this came the adoption of practices from other sports, particularly the use of chalk and training routines.

All this activity was reported in regular climbing magazines, which specifically promoted new areas to climb as well as reporting new routes. The numbers climbing became significant enough for pressure to be put on local councils to include artificial climbing walls in new sports centres. In turn, this led to a massive expansion in the numbers of young people coming into the sport through organized activities.

When The Foundry opened in Sheffield towards the end of 1990 – as a commercial climbing wall with the aim of making money – it needed 30,000 user-visits in its first year to be a viable enterprise. Colour-coded hand- and footholds make the climbing here more rigidly documented than any guidebook can, and there were many critics who felt that the reduction of adventure and increasing emphasis on gymnastic ability, coupled with an entry fee, was a recipe for financial failure. The Foundry actually received over 75,000 visitors in its first year – a reflection of how big climbing had become.

The Foundry's popularity not only mirrors the expansion of climbing, but also its diversity. For, despite all the developments over the past century, there are still people who go out with little knowledge and tackle inhospitable looking gullies with all the enthusiasm and audacity of the early pioneers. At the same time as The Foundry was catering for a new generation of urban climbers – many of whom will never climb on natural rock (which is increasingly common) – the sea-cliffs of Range West in south Pembrokeshire were being explored without any information at all. And while a number of areas of the country finally produced up-to-date guidebooks in the early 1990s, there are still places like the Lleyn peninsula that remain essentially out of the public domain.

Although I admit I will probably never climb Tennis Shoe in tennis shoes on a snowy February day ever again, I still have days that provide the same sort of thrill. One summer's day a few years ago, I climbed Il Duce at Tintagel with Bob and Australian Andy. I can still vividly remember seeing the route for the first time and being completely dumbstruck by Littlejohn's vision in attempting such a ludicrous climb. We sat shaking our heads on the platform beneath the roof, occasionally looking up, glancing at each other and then bursting out laughing: 'He must have been off his trolley!' The subsequent ascent was almost irrelevant. Somehow that atmosphere just doesn't exist at a climbing wall.

The range and variety of climbing in Britain is such that most tastes can be catered for. Routes that require high levels of gymnastic skill often lack some of the aspects of adventure – if danger is an aspect of adventure – found on more traditional routes. They may be better protected and require a number of attempts to complete, whereas there are many traditional routes that can be attempted only once. This does not devalue 'sport climbing', it merely recognizes that the challenges involved are different in the two areas.

Only in the late 1980s and early 1990s did the one style start to encroach on the other, with the widespread use of the expansion bolt. Bolts potentially eliminate danger from any route, and they can remove the necessity to climb within one's ability. They can encourage people to try routes that they will not be able to do (e.g., the scenes at Malham of recent years); they can make the experience of climbing purely a physical one (albeit requiring tremendous levels of willpower) rather than an adventurous one. Placing bolts in routes can change their character, and can therefore change the experience of climbing those routes.

There are areas in France where every route has been bolted, which has resulted in a narrowing of options there for future climbers. So far in Britain, bolts have been kept to tightly defined areas, but it is no secret that certain individuals are putting bolts elsewhere in an attempt to push forward the boundaries of these areas. Developments at Portland suggest that wholesale retro-bolting of areas may well become acceptable, and I still can't reconcile the fun I have had there with the distaste I feel for its implications elsewhere. I have always had a strong sense of the history of climbing, and I do feel that there are some routes where a sense of the past can make for a more rewarding experience: uniformly spaced bolt protection destroys that element completely. It is obvious that we are at a crucial stage in the evolution of British climbing, with whole areas, like Portland, being redeveloped with bolt protection. All writers have a duty to comment on the times they live in, and I have not shied from doing so.

We are in an age of both mass-produced climbs and an efficient media to promote them. How, then, to select Classic Rock Climbs? What is the nature of the average climber today? How have they come into the sport? What are their aspirations? What other books are they likely to buy or, indeed, have they bought?

After many arguments, I settled on keeping the routes primarily in the Hard Very Severe and Extreme grades. While acknowledging that there are innumerable fine and deserving routes in the lower grades, many of these are already over-described, and I believe most climbers aspire to at least the HVS/E1 grade nowadays. The exact choice of routes is primarily an attempt to stress variety of experience, although it has allowed me to draw out certain historical themes. The general pattern has been to describe a number of routes in an area, each offering something different and the whole covering a range of difficulty.

Many people suggested ideas for chapters that I liked tremendously and they are as valid as the arbitrary choice I have finally made. Suggestions included 'A "V" day at Tremadog', all the climbs at Tremadog whose names begin with V, in a day; the 31 three-star routes at Stanage (1983 guide); and a day out in the Lancashire quarries, at Back Bowden Doors, on Dartmoor. Other suggestions involved 'connecting' climbs; Sunset Crack, Octo and Shrike on Clogwyn du'r Arddu gives as fine a series of cumulatively difficult pitches as any other climb on the cliff – started early they maximize the use of the sun as well! Sadly, there was neither room nor time enough to cover them all.

What I have tried to do is concentrate on 'outcrop' climbs (although Beachy Head could barely be described as an 'outcrop') rather than 'mountain' routes, as previous climbing books have covered the mountain areas exceptionally well. This is the reason for the thin coverage of those traditional bastions of rock climbing, Snowdonia and the Lake District. As discussed later, I firmly disagree that popularity is induced by publicity: perhaps the reverse is often true, for however much you tell people that the Little Orme is the best place in the world, it remains hugely unpopular! I regret that I eventually left out the North York Moors, a vastly underrated area, and I am similarly pleased to have forsaken Yorkshire Gritstone. There are too many great routes in Pembroke to choose ones you would all agree with, hence the slightly quirky choice there. In some cases, the company may have been more important than the climb, but I often find that the two go together.

The result, I hope, is more than just a book about a set number of climbs, rather a book to help you extend your ideas of what climbing can be about. Great climbs can be found all over the country, but only by those who are prepared to look.

Paul Dearden
Tideswell
Derbyshire

SOUTH WALES

Ogmore

- **LOCATION** • The cliffs at Ogmore are situated between Ogmore-by-Sea and Southerndown, on the B4524, easily reached from Junction 35 on the M4. Park at a grassy area marked by concrete posts just past the Southerndown boundary sign, next to the Old Stable Tea Shop.

- **ROUTES** • Exposure Explosion HVS 5a, Phaser E3 5c, Spellbinder E4 6a.

- **FIRST ASCENTS** • Exposure Explosion – Phil Thomas, Clive Horsfield (1974); Phaser – Pat Littlejohn, John Harwood (1977); Spellbinder – Pat Littlejohn, Andy Sharp (1977).

- **CONSIDERATIONS** • The tide is the biggest factor; Exposure Explosion apart, the whole cliff is tidal, and there are many sections where escape would be difficult. Telephone 0792 366534 for details of the tides. Although rock and protection are generally good, an adventurous spirit is essential.

- **GUIDEBOOK** • *Gower and South East Wales*, ed. Alun Richardson (South Wales Mountaineering Club, 1992).

'I WENT to Ogmore – once!' There are a number of crags that are prone to this sort of sarcasm, but Ogmore seems to reap it consistently. A relatively small sea-cliff stuck on to a coastline of sand-dunes and retirement homes just south of Bridgend, it is one of those places you have to work at to get to like. There are all sorts of reasons why you can have a very bad time there, and avoiding each of these in turn provides the excitement necessary to have a great time.

Finding the crag is easy; follow any road atlas to Ogmore-by-Sea and then head out of the village towards Southerndown. After a cattle-grid and a couple of bends, the sign for Southerndown is passed, and immediately afterwards a parking spot on the right can be seen, at the top of a grassy gully running down to the sea. The house on the bend here is actually the Old Stable Tea Shop, which provides suitable food and drink before or after climbing. A quick sprint down the gully will find you at the top of the crag, next to the pinnacle that marks the start of Exposure Explosion. If you are very lucky, you will have arrived about two hours before high tide, and it will be very obvious that walking along beneath the crag will be impossible. This might make you think you have got out of climbing, as for most of its length Ogmore plunges straight into the sea at high tide, and the sea can cover up to 20 feet of the routes. However, this is what makes Exposure Explosion such a special route. At the lowly grade of HVS, it starts and ends at the top of the crag, and it makes the perfect introduction to all things Ogmorian.

Gear up next to the pinnacle, and plan carefully who is to lead the first pitch. Basically, from a belay behind the pinnacle, the leader steps through the gap and then climbs down left (facing in) to an obvious crack; easy so far. At the foot of the crack it becomes apparent that you are above a roof, and the only continuation is a chimney that leads down through the roof to a restricted stance, above yet another roof. Clearly, both leader and second should be competent at placing runners, but it is the second who has the demanding task of 'reversing' this 4a pitch. My introduction to Ogmore was as a second, and as I stepped down into the chimney, with just the sea below, I couldn't but help feel that we were on an incredibly serious route.

As it happens, the next pitch (4b or so) is less exposed, being on a wall rather than between roofs, but with the sea coming in below, you should still have a bit of excitement. The climbing follows one of the numerous horizontal bedding planes, and the rock at this level is peculiar, both feeling a little greasy in most conditions and occasionally a little flaky too. Reasonable protection is available though, especially if a full rack of Friends is carried. The second pitch ends at a good stance on the right arête of the wall. A quick look round the corner will increase the tension rapidly. The next pitch, almost always damp, climbs round the arête and into the back of a square-cut green and ugly cave, the Wet Look cave. The position here feels very committing: there are possible escapes, but if you have left the guidebook behind you won't feel too keen on taking any of the upward lines.

Escaping from the cave is no easier than gaining it. A hand traverse along the right wall and a couple of easier moves down land you on ledges, and for the first time you can really start to enjoy yourself, particularly as you still have to watch your partner getting scared! Across the lip of the cave, a thin beam of rock is suspended, making an even more exciting alternative for a strong party. You are now on easier terrain, with the sea feeling less threatening, and much easier climbing leads right to an arête. From here you get an excellent view of Tiger Bay, with the Sorcery wall on the left and the Fire wall on the right. Escape upwards is now possible, but press on around the arête at the same level and into a deep corner chimney at the left edge of the Sorcery wall. From here a final, though crux, pitch remains. Traverse right strenuously for about 15 feet and then head up for the top with the help of a large flake. As you lie on the top, drained but exhilarated, you know that this route is what climbing is all about. For those who have not been satisfied by Exposure Explosion, or if the tide has not started to go out by then, an excellent continuation is to drop down the final chimney about ten feet and then traverse across the wall to the right for a further two long pitches, a Bigger Splash. This good value E3 5b, 5b combines very strenuous climbing across the main part of the Sorcery wall, with some thrilling moments above the huge cave at the back of the bay.

Having got a taste of the Ogmore atmosphere, and suitably fortified with blackcurrant pancakes from the tea shop above, it is now time to get down to sea-level. On a first visit, it is probably best to explore the area beneath Exposure Explosion, as this is the easiest to escape from if the sea or weather threatens. The descent is down Route One (a Difficult), that is easily found some 80 yards right (looking out to sea) of the pinnacle. A rocky platform, with two iron stakes in it, marks the top, and the corner leading up to the left-hand side (looking out) of the platform is both solid rock and easily down climbed. The bottom of this section of cliff can be traversed safely for about two hours either side of low tide, if the sea is fairly calm. Working back right from Route One (facing in), there are a number of very obvious corners and grooves, and it is well worth doing a number of the easier routes (such as Pluto, VS) to help get the feel of the place. The classic Pinnochio (HVS) is also very worth while. It finishes at the pinnacle, making it a good route to end on. Before leaving though, have another look around that arête at Tiger Bay. Except at low tide, you will need to roll up your trousers and boulder hop round to it, but it is well worth the effort so that you can take in the lines of Spellbinder, Daughter of Regals and Warlock on the Sorcery Wall, as well as the ludicrous cave at the back of the bay and its future lines. If time permits, you can scramble across the beach past the castle, a small stack, and a very dodgy-looking area of rock, Hob Nob Bay, all the way to Davy Jones' Locker. This is the venue for a number of superb-looking Martin Crocker routes, including the stunning 45-foot roof that forms pitch two of Davy Jones' Locker itself – a route that must rank as one of the most spectacular in the country, particularly as it will inevitably involve the second either drowning, or at the very least, having to climb the horizontal roof with the sea directly below, should the leader not be quick. The toe of the buttress forming the right edge of the cave is rarely passable without getting wet, so that is probably enough looking for now, and you had better get back while you still can.

Now that you have got some bearings, a second visit should be productive, but just to add an air of uncertainty, and to keep the excitement up, you ought to start with a route you haven't seen yet: Phaser. This lies some 20 yards to the right of the buttress right of Davy Jones' Locker, and it needs to be approached in one of two ways. If you are not staying long, or fancy a full day exploring, then continue along the road into Southerndown itself and take an unsigned right turn down to Dunraven Bay. This is a bit of a beauty spot, so expect crowds on a sunny day. From here, the eastern end of Ogmore can be explored by walking along the beach for about three hours either side of low tide. There are a number of unusual routes here, like the Hunchback (a bizarre E1) and even more odd rock. The three large slabs forming the bulk of this end of the crag are on rock that is no better than it looks, and they should be avoided; but left of them (looking in), and just before the impasse, is a very impressive wall littered with roofs and bulging all over. This is Phaser wall and its eponymous route is a sensational E3. This crag can also be reached from the tea shop by following the edge of the cliff and looking out for Davy Jones' Locker. There are a number of stakes in place just past the cave, and abseiling from these should get you past the impasse.

Phaser is the obvious line on the wall, a clean crack-line that appears to bulge slightly from a distance. Close up, you realize that it is actually more like a roof, with the first 30 feet overhanging at least 15 feet. Although this lower section provides what is probably the technical crux (at 5c), it is safe and you are still fresh. Superb crozzly rock makes for painful finger jams, and the movements have to be swift and positive. Once round the bulge though, copious big footholds help take the strain, but only at the expense of the rock reverting to the stratified horizontal limestone. The remainder of the pitch is just a battle between mind, body and gravity. The runners are good, but they are sparse in places; and the holds are good, but it is steep; so have faith, try to blot out the emotions and keep pulling. Resting is not advised, as the pitch seems to go on for ever. Just below the top, a couple of harder moves (probably only 5b in reality) threaten to spurn you, but grit your teeth and trust the edge of the crack as you layback past them. Take a set of Friends, and save some large nuts for the upper section.

By now you will either be a convert or never want to come here again. Do be warned that Phaser's E3 5c grade will seem stiff, but that is why some acclimatization is needed here. The routes tend to pack a lot into their meagre length, and commitment and a confident approach is everything. Nowhere is this better illustrated than on the walls of Tiger Bay, where good rock combines with bold steep climbing to create a number of classics. Virtually all of the routes are worth while, with Spellbinder (at E4 6a) being one of the very best.

Once you know your way around a bit, you can abseil into Tiger Bay from stakes above the Fire wall, and you get about two hours either side of low tide, depending on the route, to climb here. It is really important here – more than on the easier routes – that you come to climb in good conditions. With the starts of all these routes being underwater for much of the time, there is a high tendency for the holds to be greasy, particularly where the rock is very compact. Low tide needs to be combined with afternoon sun for a worthwhile visit, and a breeze is often helpful. Given that failure on a route here could result in wet feet, it is probably worth carrying jumars as well, or at the very least identifying possible escape routes: The Bishop and Siren (at HVS and VS) are the easiest, being the leftmost and rightmost lines respectively. It is quite possible to be cut off from them though, so be careful. Spellbinder takes a strong natural line across and then up the Sorcery wall, starting at the first obvious break right of the chimney of Siren, and following the obvious rightwards-trending ramp-line past a long, deep horizontal slot, before finishing directly up the bulging head-wall above A Bigger Splash.

The lower section is on immaculate rock, and it needs to be fairly dry to get your confidence up. Smooth scoops and crozzly finger jugs lead up steeply to the deep slot, and good protection makes the whole thing seem enjoyable. Strenuous moves up and right find another slot, more runners and a long look at the next few moves. The trick is not to look too long and just go for it. Within moments you will either be grasping jugs in the break of A Bigger Splash or hanging on the rope some 15 feet below. No place to pause, but focus your concentration at least, because you are still going up, even though there is a very unlikely looking bulging wall above! From here on, it is really just jug pulling, but the sense of exposure grows with every move, and the angle is hideous, with no rests for 20 feet. You will soon know if you are into Ogmore mode or not. Once wedged against the detached block, the strenuousness eases a little, but mentally it is still demanding; the ledges above feel commodious, and the arête above seems so much easier after a brief rest.

Not perhaps one of the crags you'd like to be stuck with on a desert island, but despite the tides, the rock and the humble length of the routes, you can get into climbing at Ogmore. If you do, then you will know when it is time to go there again, and when you are in that sort of mood there are few places that can be so rewarding.

Gower

■ **LOCATION** • Yellow Wall, at the back of Great Boulder Cove, between Fall Bay and Mewslade Bay, approached from Rhossili.

- ■ *ROUTES* • Transformer (E3 5c), Yellow Wall (E3 5c), Yellow Regeneration (E5 6b).

- ■ *FIRST ASCENTS* • Transformer – Pat Littlejohn, A. McFarlane (1973), Chris King, Steve Monks (1978); Yellow Wall – Pat Littlejohn, A. Houghton (1973); Yellow Regeneration – Martin Crocker, Roy Thomas, Matt Ward (1986).

- ■ *CONSIDERATIONS* • Yellow Wall is home to many sea-birds during the nesting season, and there is a ban on climbing between 1 March and 10 August inclusive. The wall gets any available sun for a good part of the day, and it is in a remarkably sheltered position.

- ■ *GUIDEBOOK* • Gower and South East Wales , ed. Alun Richardson (South Wales Mountaineering Club, 1992).

GOWER WAS the first region in Britain to be designated an 'Area of Outstanding Natural Beauty', and in a reasonably compact area it offers rock climbers a marvellous combination of physical exercise and spiritual relaxation. A pleasant stroll across a perfect beach often forms the warm-up to excellent climbing, with a number of non-tidal possibilities within walking distance should the seas be against you. Apart from the beauty of the coastline itself, which is less rugged than the south Cornwall coast but seamed with equally fine beaches, the cliffs have much to commend them. The rock is a superb grey limestone, dappled yellow with lichens on some of the least-frequented cliffs, but of almost perfect quality in many places, reminiscent of the best parts of Yorkshire limestone cliffs. Add to this the generally short nature of the cliffs, rarely reaching a rope length, and the slabby angle of many cliffs, and you can understand why Gower must be one of the finest venues for middle-grade climbers in South Wales, with a huge number of routes in the Severe to HVS grades.

Certainly, Gower is unusual in that it offers clean, solid limestone routes in the easier grades that are very worth while, and the polish on some of the original classics, like Dulfer at Boiler Slab, proves that this is where Gower's popularity has always lain. However, the surge in free-climbing standards throughout the 1970s and 1980s did not bypass Gower, although the majority of climbers in Britain do not seem to have realized this. Indeed, tucked away among the many small buttresses and coves that line the south coast of the Gower peninsula are some of the finest – and hardest – climbs in South Wales, comparable to the very best Pembroke routes.

The main area for free-climbing, and an area of national importance in climbing terms, is the stretch of coast between Fall Bay and Thurba

Head, at the very tip of the peninsula. If you are fortunate or clever enough to arrive at Rhossili when the tide is going out, you can explore this part from the beach, making an enjoyable day out in itself! As two of the major cliffs, Yellow Wall and Thurba Head itself, are subject to bird restrictions, they can only be climbed on in the autumn and winter months, from mid August to the end of February. A fine summer's day when you feel too tired to climb, or even a miserable drizzling day escaping from Pembroke, makes a good time to familiarize yourself with the approaches and take stock of some of the lines. The routes around the Giant's Cave are unrestricted and look easier in the warm glow of a summer's day; only the numerous bathers and Scout groups that accompany fine weather detract slightly from the perfect setting.

Approaching from the car-park in Rhossili – which is not as easy as it should be – the first crag you meet is the impressively positioned Fall Bay Buttress. Well above the sea, but often catching a wind, this buttress has a number of excellent VS routes, as well as a good E2 5b (Seth) that take the distinct steep, jamming crack followed by the roof at its widest part. Traversing around the foot of this buttress leads you to a ramp running down to the beach, and to the gaping hole of the Giant's Cave.

The routes here are all obvious lines, many with some *in situ* gear to help the eye along. The conspicuous white, dramatically leaning, arête is Pat Littlejohn's Masterpiece, a bold and strenuous E6 6b. It is well worth checking the section above the break by first doing Thriller (E4 6a), a good route that climbs the unmistakable crack just inside the cave, before swinging out into the common hanging groove above the leaning arête. Can't Buy a Thrill (E5 6b) follows the same crack, but it comes straight out over the roof instead of escaping leftwards, and is a good precursor to the remaining two routes. Both of these climb the roof of the cave itself, finishing out of the blow-hole! Jesus Wept (E6 6a) – a typical Pete Oxley creation – climbs from the very back of the cave, with a tricky start (jumping does help) followed by amazingly good holds on a rightwards-trending line. The remaining route is a Martin Crocker creation, The Divine Guiding Light. This stunning E7 6b climbs the thin crack and flake towards the back of the left-hand wall, and then swings up and left-wards to the roof, which is climbed across to a chimney and an awkward exit into the blow-hole; clearly an outrageous piece of climbing, but very safe, and a realistic challenge for the strong.

For all its impressive climbing though, the Giant's Cave is just a side-show compared to Yellow Wall. Here the cliffs reach their full height of 150 feet, and this impressive wall now holds over a dozen superb routes – in a cove which forms a perfect setting. When the sea cuts off retreat, it is possible to scramble out (or in) from the other side of the cove, so although access is restricted because of the birds nesting, it is rare to find the wall inaccessible because of the tide. First appearances suggest that the wall is steep but don't really prepare you for how steep.

In the centre of the wall is a superb overhung corner, blatantly the line of the crag: this is Yellow Wall. To the right, a long groove line slants up rightwards, forming the first pitch of Transformer, while Yellow Regeneration takes the rock that actually does look steep to the right of this! Although there are some easier routes on the cliff, the most satisfying ones are all E3 or above, with Transformer providing probably the best introduction to the climbing.

The groove of Transformer is undercut at its base, and the start instantly tells you what you are in for: brilliant holds, good natural protection and very steep rock! Climb the bulge quickly and boldly, with the prospect of a reasonable rest next to good Friends above, although it is possible to boulder up and fix a thread if you are less confident in your arms. The groove is rarely technical; a few short sections requiring unsubtle bridging in order to connect the best handholds; and it would present no difficulties at all if only it were vertical. But it is not, and you realize very soon that your eyes have been deceived by the angle of the cliff. Fortunately, relief arrives as the groove doglegs left, and some easier angled ground, requiring thought and technique, leads to a well-positioned ledge.

A thoughtful second will give you plenty of time to recover before the more strenuous top pitch. This is shorter but probably steeper, and certainly more technical. The groove-line continues to a short bulge, and some committing moves past antique ironmongery to the base of a deep crack. This is followed to the top, with a combination of jamming and thrutching being the best technique. It is possible to escape out left from the crack into an easier groove. A few potentially loose blocks at the top of the crack suggests that this is what most parties do, so if your energy banks are running low, you can feel justified in taking this alternative on environmental grounds.

Although also graded E3 5c, Yellow Wall is a good grade harder than Transformer! Together they represent opposite ends of both the E grade and technical grade spectra. Indeed, a strong and confident leader might well dismiss Transformer at E2 5b without being too precocious, whereas many run-of-the-mill leaders would want to upgrade Yellow Wall! The route starts beneath a groove running down from a triangular roof, which stops short of reaching the ground. A funny move – stepping off a boulder and just trusting that the base of the groove is full of holds – is required to start. Once you are bridged in the groove, which is already steep, you feel unusually committed for ten feet of climbing. Of course, the back of the groove supplies plentiful holds and wire runners, and everything proceeds without incident to the roof. A long sling needs to be placed on any gear below the roof, as the rope drag incurred otherwise will make the crux particularly tricky. As you approach the roof, a deep crack on the left wall becomes very useful, and shuffling left in the break beneath the roof leads to an exposed arête. The holds are enormous though, and it is easy to pull up into a curious cave for a good rest.

Above the cave, the difficulty escalates. A superb thread can be fixed in the roof of the cave before peeping out for a look. Above is a blank wall, below the void beneath the triangular roof, and some ten feet up to the right, hidden from sight around a blunt arête, is the obvious corner that provides the line. Two pegs, although only one is serviceable, protect a technical sequence first up, on small fingerholds, then right on to a layaway on the arête. Blindly reaching round, a positive flake can be felt, and you just have to commit yourself to swinging round on to it, hoping the holds stay good. They do, and although you have to climb and forget about runners, the corner, good wires and a wide bridging rest soon appear.

The position here is very dramatic: you have cut back above the roof and turned an arête from the cave, so both your ropes disappear from view very quickly. Your second will need to be standing well out from the rock to be visible too. The steepest part is yet to come. Climb the corner: a mixture of laybacking and poor jams, with the odd ridiculous bridging position to place gear. I once saw a photo of a climber on Amen Corner, Gimmer Crag, where it appeared that both faces of the corner overhung, and this bold soul was laybacking, feet almost above his head, with no runners and a hemp rope trailing behind. When I got to Amen Corner some years later, it was, of course, a disappointment. But here, on Yellow Wall, I think I came as close as it is possible to sharing that moment with the climber in that photograph. My hands didn't fit for jamming, the crack being awkwardly between hand and finger size, and my legs were not long enough to bridge out of trouble. So, throwing a few Friends in, and secured to two modern ropes, I put my feet above my head and laybacked, and it felt every bit as desperate and serious as it looked in the climber's face in the photo.

The reward for this labour is a very palatial ledge, equipped with stones which you can use to test the angle of the rock you have just come up! A delicate and quite bold top pitch, that is probably harder than it feels (but it is such a relief to climb the right side of vertical again), soon leads to the top, and good belays well up the slope.

Both Transformer and Yellow Wall are as good as they come; while for those who revel in steep rock, the section of wall to the right boasts three classy E6 routes, all strenuous but basically safe.

Yellow Regeneration was the first of these routes to be done, and it is probably the best, having a little more variety and a better line than the other two. It packs plenty of drama into a relatively short first pitch that powers its way up the centre of the steepest section, the odd thread and peg giving you something to go for, but still requiring plenty of tenacity. A fine belay at the easing of angle allows rest for the body if not for the mind, and the second pitch is very intimidating to look at. As it happens, the positions on the second pitch are outrageous, but the climbing is reasonably steady, a couple of very long reaches/wild lunges providing the main interest up on the arête. A real test of stamina, physically and mentally, but without danger: the air is a very soft landing spot. Any competent party would be blinkered in the extreme to ignore routes like this.

Yet these routes are ignored. I climbed here at the end of a relatively dry winter season, just before the bird ban commenced for the year, and

Yellow Wall was the only line on the cliff with any evidence of chalk. From this I deduce that either there is a new breed of chalk-free climbers who are operating only at places like the Gower and Ogmore, mainly at night, or very few people actually go there! Yet the climbing is immaculate, the rock and positions superb, and the cliff south facing! How strange that this beautiful place, which is almost as much fun when you are not climbing, but just strolling along the beach, should be passed by so regularly.

Pembrokeshire

- ■ *LOCATION* • Mount Sion East in Range West, approached from the Stack Rocks car-park at the end of the road that bisects the Castlemartin Artillery Range. Space Buttress and Bosherston Head in Range East, approached from the St Govan's car park, and Stackpole Head, best approached from Stackpole Quay.

- ■ *ROUTES* • Lost in Space (HVS 5a), Planet Waves (E2 5b), Swordfish (E3 5c), Star Wars (E4 5c).

- ■ *FIRST ASCENTS* • Lost in Space – Paul Donnithorne, Emma Alsford, Dave Viggars (1992); Planet Waves – Pat Littlejohn, Charlie Heard (1980) Steve Monks, Damian Carroll (1984); Swordfish – P. Littlejohn, Chris King (1978); Star Wars – Ben and Marion Wintringham, C. Heard (1980).

- ■ *CONSIDERATIONS* • Three of these routes are in the Castlemartin Artillery Range and access is subject to various by-laws; further details in the text. In addition, Swordfish is in an area of importance to nesting sea birds, and must be avoided between 1 March and 15 August.

- ■ *GUIDEBOOKS* • Pembroke by Jon de Montjoye and Mike Harber (Climbers' Club, 1985); a new edition, in two or three parts, is planned for 1995. A *RockFax Selected Climbs* guide is also planned for 1995.

PEMBROKE MEANS so many different things to me. It is famous for sun and sea, crowds crawling over baking rock, busy bars and car-parks, and breakfast at Ma Weston's. Holiday climbing is the theme, with eating out and even beach parties all part of the scene. The scale of gatherings at some Easters is so immense, it is hard to believe that there is anyone left to go to Stanage, but, of course, that too will be crowded. However, arrive on a Monday, out of peak season, and more often than not Pembroke is empty; add a thick sea mist, a coat of salt on the holds and you are on your own.

Pembroke is such a large climbing area that there is always something new to discover and always something familiar to fall back on, and the majority of the routes are of an amazingly high quality. It is easy to pick off three-star routes on a weekend, and it never seems possible to catch up with the next batch being produced! Pembroke is also a place for the extraordinary, for surprises. There are so many 'unusual' routes that the unusual has become the commonplace, and adjectives become meaningless.

For a start, there is the neat distinction between the north coast and the south coast. The north coast has a completely different atmosphere; with its unusual rock, it has some of the feel of its Devon counterpart: some open slabs mixed in with broody, gloomy cliffs with some very serious routes for their lowly grades. The south coast, mile after mile of steep limestone, is more popular, and justly so, though most visitors restrict themselves to a very narrow stretch of the coastline. Then there are the 'features': The Cauldron, a collapsed sea-cave that provides one of the most interesting sea-level explorations around; the bizarre formation of Huntsman's Leap, home to a number of brilliant routes; the unusual chimney of Deep Space; the magnificent sheet of the White Tower, and so many more. With such a vast amount of rock to go at, it seems difficult to choose a limited number of climbs: there are stacks of great E5s that all deserve recognition, but many of those are in popular areas and likely to come under a visitor's scrutiny without any further encouragement. It is in the lower to middle extreme grades that Pembroke holds some less well known gems.

The early 1990s were interesting times in Pembroke. Climbers had known of the four miles of cliff that lie between Linney Head and the Elegug stacks for many years, and the odd route had been done secretly. This area, Range West, was strictly out of bounds to climbers though, being a live firing range for the MoD. A cleverly fought PR campaign, together with a wider leaking of information about what routes had already been done in the Range, eventually culminated in a mass trespass on 20 October 1991. The MoD was forced to discuss the possibility of climbing if it was to avoid numerous repeats of these scenes, and so an access agreement had been drawn up by the start of the following year. Although the conditions the army laid down were difficult to take seriously, many climbers took advantage of the new arrangements with grace and patience, and 1992 proved to be a bumper year for new routeing.

Having missed the first 'recruiting' day, at which prospective climbers were briefed, screened and tied up in red tape, I made my first visit as the guest of an authorized climber. This in itself involved filling in countless forms, including one that promised I would stay close to my leader! However, approached in a spirit of good humour, it was all good fun, and we were soon 'out on the Range'.

The first thing you notice about the cliffs in Range West is that the bedding planes that are so prominent in the rest of Pembroke are not nearly so straight and regular. There has been much more folding in the formation of these rocks, and so the clifftop is less even, and the actual rock itself more varied than along the coast. Consequently, it is a more exciting place to explore than the reasonably uniform Range East, with many of the cliffs being accessible without abseil.

Very keen to get involved in the new routeing scene, we spent a frustrating day starting up numerous new lines, retreating from all of them. The established ethic in Range West is ground up exploration, with no abseil inspection and no pre-placed gear, of any kind. This means no belay stakes as well, which the MoD claims is a necessary precaution, given the number of unexploded shells lying around! Such new routeing is firmly within the traditions of rock climbing in Britain, but the sort of commitment it required was beyond us. You could not help but be impressed by the contributions of other climbers though, venturing on to all sorts of ridiculous-looking ground with no prior knowledge at all.

Although enjoyable enough, we soon tired of our continual failure, and determined to repeat some of the existing routes. With only a few scribbled notes for reference, we were attracted by the sound of Lost in Space, as much by its grade as its unusual description. This bizarre climb is much more fun than it ought to be – in other words, it has little to do with climbing, but is more in the way of an 'experience'. Mount Sion East is an extensive crag, the top of which is easily identifiable by the abseil hole that forms the easiest descent. The hole, some 30 feet back from the edge, sits like a manhole in the base of a little level platform that makes an ideal place to gear up. Abseiling down the hole is amusing in itself, especially for larger members of the party, and it is well worth going slowly and taking in your surroundings. The hole is actually the blow-hole of a large cave, and after a few feet you are in space, although the main roof of the cave is at a lower level: the roof has a higher chamber with the blow-hole at its top. As you descend, look out to sea; there is actually a passage running out from this chamber to the main cliff face above the roof! Lost in Space takes this horizontal passage.

The foot of Mount Sion East is very accessible in calm seas, but in rough conditions the rock shelves that form the base of the crag seem to funnel waves on to the rock, and it is easy to get caught out. There are a number of impressive lines in this area: the superb Diedre, amazingly only E2, being one of the best; but Lost in Space is so enjoyable it has to be the first route done. Starting beneath the huge cave, a relatively easy crack and corner leads up into the roof, and an impasse level with the passageway. Here you can either throw yourself dramatically around the corner into the start of the passageway, heaving on sloping but large holds, or drop down slightly and make a few more technical but less committing moves round to the same point.

Once in the passage, the route is clear: crawl to the light. At the end, it is possible to squirm out on to the head-wall, and an instant 80 feet of exposure! Runners are unnecessary, as you have effectively just threaded the roof. A short wall, at no more than Severe standard, provides a fitting finale for such an interesting route. Taking a bit of care to arrange runners at the top of the cave, it is actually possible to belay looking down the blow-hole, although there is a lot of loose material at the cliff edge, and care needs to be taken not to dislodge these rocks.

Returning to Range East soon after my first visit into Range West, the first thing that struck me was the way so many climbers congregate within such a short distance of the car-park. Yet there are some real gems just a little further into the Range – Planet Waves being one of my favourites. An unlikely looking route, in an unfrequented area, it offers plenty of excitement and variety in its two pitches. The best approach is by a direct abseil down the route; this gives you a belay at the top and a longer access time at the foot. Ropes should be pulled for maximum effect, as the small cove beneath the crag is soon cut off by an incoming sea.

The first pitch takes in a thuggy roof, on excellent juggy holds. Yet it is harder than it looks: the problem being that not all the holds on the short wall above the roof are jugs, and energy can be easily wasted sorting them out. The first time I did Planet Waves, my partner kept falling off once he had got round the roof, and his determination not to be beaten almost got me wet feet! From the belay, the excellent second pitch can be surveyed – a perfect steep slab of grey rock, with generally good holds, especially where it steepens, and a not too generously protected feeling. Intricate route finding, with good rests and a 'lonely' feel combine to make this route a classic E2, and one I have enjoyed again and again.

Of course, there is more to climbing in Pembroke than the Castlemartin Ranges. The massive quantity of rock near Lydstep is home to some sensational routes, including the very popular ones at Mother Carey's Kitchen. The recent developments in Raming Hole and the more traditional Mowing Word are also gaining popularity. One cliff that sees very little attention though, despite a wealth of existing and future classics, is the very steep West face of Stackpole Head. Bird restricted, with no climbing between the end of February and mid-August, it is rare to arrive there and find somebody on your intended route; which may not be surprising because it has some wild climbing in exciting positions! Abseiling in – necessary only if the tide has not fully exposed the boulders beneath the crag – helps you to appreciate the angle, and makes you realize you should have brought those prussik loops.

Many of the routes here are excellent, but the stunning line of Swordfish takes some beating. The striking groove above the roofs in the centre of the cliff provides a brilliant outing, technically easy for 5c, but fully deserving its E3. Starting up the wonderfully barnacled rock, the climbing is straightforward, if steep, to the roof. An undercut wall runs leftwards. This is followed, with one tricky move that can be avoided with a cunning hand change, to the base of the main groove. The exposure here feels much greater than it should, the 50 feet or so above the boulders accentuated greatly for the second if the tide has started to race in! Some quick pulls get you established in the groove, and a semi-rest on a ledge on the left. The technical crux follows, with a difficult sequence left of the main groove finishing at a good hold, and a step back into the groove. This is followed to the top on good holds. A possible belay below the top probably eases rope drag, and will certainly aid communication.

It is almost impossible to single out routes that represent such a vast area as Pembroke. There are routes of a very committing nature, where the sea is a crucial factor, but many that are barely more than climbs by the sea. The climbing is generally steep, and natural protection normally good. Every cliff seems to have at least one classic! However, even among such quality there is one route that seems to capture the very best aspects of Pembroke climbing very succinctly: Star Wars. This superb face climb, hidden away at the junction of Bosherston Head and Huntsman's Leap, but not visible or accessible from either, has it all: a committing abseil approach, requiring some thought to set up; a tide-affected start, with the second regularly ending up covered in spray; bold open-face climbing (although with good protection where it counts); and a superb position, particularly in the upper section.

The route can be seen from two different positions, either side of Huntsman's Leap. From the east side of the leap you get an excellent picture of the face, with the ledge at its foot easily seen if the tide is low. The abseil approach can be spotted from here, just left of the corner. Going round to the west side of the Leap gives a completely different view. Suddenly the angle of the face seems to have tilted, although this is in fact an illusion. Abseiling down to the ledge, you feel in a remarkably lonely position, considering the proximity to two of the busiest crags in Range East. The route begins up the corner for ten feet, and then traces a stepped line out and upwards, following the best holds on the wall. Nowhere is the climbing very hard, although the short section above and right of the horizontal break is certainly 5c, but the atmosphere makes the whole route feel serious and sustained. Good wires can be placed where they are most needed, but a confident approach is very helpful towards the top. A lack of confidence in the leader can have damp consequences for the second, and it is certainly not a route that either climber should start falling off, hence the E4 grade overall.

To be a pioneer and come across something like Star Wars, or any of the other routes, and to climb them on sight, unsure of what is to come, must be the greatest thrill that climbing can offer; that is why access to Range West is so important, and why the strict ethic adopted there is so commendable, for only in this way will future climbers be able to share that feeling.

The Valleys

■ *LOCATION* •Cwmaman Main Quarry, on the hillside above Cwmaman, just off the A4275 Aberdare to Mountain Ash road; Dinas Rock, in the woods upriver from Pont Nedd Fechan, two miles north-east of Glyn Neath.

■ *ROUTES* • Mother of Pearl (E4 6b), Spain (E4 6a), Berlin (E5 6b).

■ *FIRST ASCENTS* • Mother Of Pearl – Andy Sharp, P. Lewis (1988); Spain – Gary Gibson (1985); Berlin – Gary Gibson, Martin Crocker (1985) .

■ *CONSIDERATIONS* • The rock at Cwmaman is fairly clean, quarried sandstone; Mother of Pearl is quick drying and gets plenty of sun. Park considerately just below the quarry! Dinas Rock is formed of high quality, if sometimes a little dusty, limestone, and the two routes here are fairly unaffected by rain.

■ *GUIDEBOOK* • *Gower and South East Wales,* ed. Alun Richardson (South Wales Mountaineering Club, 1992).

THE VALLEYS of South Wales contain a plethora of cliffs, both on natural and quarried rock, on limestone and gritstone. In all these places it is difficult to single out really memorable routes of less than an E3 standard, so I make no apologies for the chosen routes in this area all being so hard. There are good easier routes, like Phobia at Morlais, an interesting water-washed groove that gives a new meaning to rounded holds, but the bulk of the easier routes lack something special. In many cases they are just not long enough to make much of position, or the nature of the rock might be such that the easier routes are inevitably on less good rock. Whatever the cause, one result is that this area provides too little to attract the HVS leader for it to be really worth recommending a detour.

What these cliffs do have, though, is an incredibly large number of essentially well-protected 'modern' climbs, and it is very surprising that the hordes of northern 'sport climbers' have not yet caught on. The valleys provide an almost futuristic vision of climbing for the sake of the movement, with a backdrop of industrial despoliation and many of the cliffs covered with humourless graffiti. Few of the cliffs themselves are memorable: the most striking memory I have of one is of a dead dog, still with its collar and lead, some 20 feet away from the foot of a 30-foot drop. Climbing that day took on a sense of urgency, all of us vowing never to return to that particular spot, and unable to look out across the valley without a peculiarly jaundiced eye.

But the valleys have got something to teach us all too. The sandstone quarries are monuments to history; each village has its own little nick in the hillside, each quarry warning us of the damage caused by a free-for-all policy of exploitation. More interestingly for climbers, the quarries give us a chance to experience that real pleasure – the square sandstone edge – that disappeared from the northern grit quarries years ago. What it must have been like to have climbed at Millstone or Froggat in the days when all those little flakes had nice square edges! Here in the valleys you can learn once again to balance on your feet without smearing: if you have ever bouldered on a badly pointed brick wall you will know just what to expect.

There is a downside to this: the climbing can be repetitive, with many routes at the same venue sharing angle, solidity, size of hold and so on. Indeed, it is possible to visit some venues without a guidebook, climb all the routes and then be unable to distinguish descriptions in the guidebook only a few days later. This fact, and the relatively copious quantities of fixed gear at most venues, make the quarries very much a muscle ground – a training paradise for some but uninspiring for others. The facts are that the small edges perfectly create routes of E3 and above – where the edges are small and mainly solid – and that the tops are often avoided by lower off points. If they were ever to get popular, you would very quickly feel a climbing-wall atmosphere at many of these quarries, which is already happening at the most popular quarry, The Gap. This is also one of the only quarries where you are likely to see other climbers, and in terms of concentration of good climbing, it is certainly the best of the quarries.

It is probably for these reasons that the one route I can distinctly remember, and which I feel sure must be among the best in the valleys, is also one of the first sandstone routes I did in the area. There is always something exciting about new areas, and that first touch is often the most sought after and passionate. I had heard murmurs about the valleys for a number of months, and then read a report in one of the magazines that seemed to suggest a massive wave of exploration and development. Finding myself near by, with partners who were easily persuadable, we headed for Gladys Quarry, armed with a few lines of information but no descriptions. Two hours later we were leaving, having crossed off the pleasant Gladys; we were unimpressed – the routes were short and overprotected. However, many of the individual moves had been good, and we were keen to give somewhere else a go. The only other place for which we had directions was Cwmaman, so we drove round, unsure whether the effort was going to be worth it. On entering the quarry, the obvious Arête Buttress appeared bigger than Gladys, but the rock looked poor (although this is a false impression). Almost immediately, another wall came into view though, and bathed in the sunshine it looked impressively unbroken. Running over with excitement, we quickly found ourselves beneath a superb piece of rock. There were a number of lines of fixed gear, the three on the steep right-hand section looking very hard indeed. We had no route information, but decided that a line just left of centre, up a vertical wall creased only by a few horizontal breaks, looked the best. Unknown to us at the time, this was Mother of Pearl.

It is such an unusual feeling to be climbing a steep wall on small positive holds with plenty of friction. So much hard limestone climbing involves layaways, undercuts, body contortions and smearing your feet with funny technical foot angles, which is why limestone is so well suited to high standard technical climbing of course; but here at Cwmaman there was a problem of a different sort: climb the wall direct, using the obvious holds in the obvious way. Brutal, direct; but still very hard! Every hold good, but every hold small, and the wall just a touch too steep; lean everything back a few degrees and you would have a wonderful 5b/c slab, probably just as fine. As it is, you use slab techniques, powerful rockovers on positive little footholds, but all the while the power meter is falling swiftly. It took me three attempts to redpoint the route, and I felt I wanted to redo it straight away. We did as much else in the quarry as we could, and left as the sun was setting, impressed, and knowing that we would be back. I haven't returned yet, although I have been to lots of the other little quarries that spring up out of the valleys; all have some good climbing to offer, but none can match Mother of Pearl.

Contrastingly, Dinas Rock is a place that I have visited many times. I first went there in 1981, visiting a friend who lived near by. Although most of the modern lines lay untouched, it was still an impressive place. The 'hidden world' aspect of the Main Overhang area was accentuated by the old bridge that used to run from the end of the path, beneath the Kennelgarth Wall, up over the waterfalls to the top path. The bridge had a danger sign draped casually over one of the railings: a superfluous notice, as the bulk of the wooden boards had disappeared, and the whole structure seemed destined to collapse at any moment! Having negotiated a way up to the 'main overhang', the roof now taken by Giant Killer and the surrounding walls were astonishing. The only route to tackle this section was the ubiquitous Springboard. This involved climbing the most dead tree I have ever seen to the lip of the roof, and then continuing at E3 6a into what appeared to be a jungle above. The tree looked E5, so I was not tempted, settling instead for the curious feature that forms Groovy Tube Day at the right-hand side of the cliff. I left with a feeling of unfinished business rather than excitement, but knowing I would be back.

When I eventually did return, things had changed. The bridge and tree had both gone, no surprises there; but what was surprising was the routes that had appeared upstream. I had seen photos of Giant Killer, and probably because I remembered how big the roof was, I was not very inspired. The sheet of perfect limestone to the right – now home to

Berlin, The Big Time and Salem's Lot – was a different matter though, and I felt an instant attraction. Unfortunately, all of its routes had hard starts, and we abandoned them after a bit of messing about and looked at Spain, written up as a 'potential classic' in the 1985 supplement.

Sharing an arboreal start with Groovy Tube Day, the climbing quickly leads you to a scoop below the tube. Ignoring this, you step out left on good holds, past the thread runners that seem to be the hallmark of Gibson routes from this era. A bulge is quickly reached, with a poor rest beneath. Above the holds are poor, and the protection in the corner above the bulge is not reassuring. Above and out on the arête, more threads beckon though, so you commit yourself to the bulge: a hard pull into the corner followed by a technical traverse right finds you beneath the threads, but there is now a little sense of urgency in the proceedings, and the position feels more committing than it probably is. Good routes get harder at this point, and Spain is no exception, although technically the crux is behind you now. Determination and strength are needed now to pass a peg on to the exposed upper wall, where a few swift pulls gain a belay sling. Although full of exhilaration, take a moment to check that the belay is adequate before lowering back down to the ground; the rope spends most of the year in the undergrowth and doesn't seem to get changed much. A fairly long length of 9 mm rope is needed to back-up or replace the belay, back to a sound tree rather than round the decaying sapling at the edge of the cliff.

It is sad that such a potential classic as Spain should not get enough traffic to warrant a regular belay renewal, but the route is still languishing in the ranks of potentials rather than actuals. What has perhaps been overlooked is that Dinas Rock provides the perfect answer to the wet Sunday in Pembroke. In the summer months you can almost guarantee climbable rock, albeit at a high standard, and if you are not up to the routes, the woods beyond the Main Overhang make an interesting change from pounding the wet clifftops in Range East! I have even taken a day out from a wet Pembroke in November with success, but never seen more than one other party in the area. I keep wanting to try The Big Time, but for two reasons I somehow never get on it! Firstly, because the route looks so hard. Secondly, because Berlin is so good that you just have to make anyone you take there do it, and that never leaves time or strength to try anything else!

There is something definitive about Berlin. It represents so well an attitude of using fixed protection prevalent briefly in the 1980s, before the gymnasts took over and moulded it for their own ends. Berlin does use two bolts, and it also has two pegs and a thread in its 70-odd feet. That is all, though, and it certainly does not feel generously protected. The boulder-problem start is frustrating for the shorter climber, but can be worked on at leisure. Once established, holds lead quickly to jugs round the first bulge, and a peg. Passing this feels committing, and the next few moves up to the first bolt are both technical and bold. The angle is reasonable, and you can work out exactly what to do before stepping up carefully. Once up, the difficulties accumulate, and more bold moves lead through a further slight bulge to the next bolt and a measure of rest. Above is a leaning groove, which looks difficult to gain. It is, and a great deal of faith is needed to commit yourself into groping almost blindly for the good holds that you feel sure should wait for you after a thin sequence of precarious moves. They are there, but the angle suddenly spits you backwards, and you must act decisively on them. When you pull over the top and clip into the sumptuous belay, you don't feel that you have been 'sport' climbing at all!

Perhaps that is why Dinas Rock has won me back so often, and why, when I bought the *Gower and South East Wales* guide, I couldn't even remember some of the sandstone quarries I had visited!

Postscript: Over the summer of 1994 Dinas Rock has seen an increase in traffic, and a number of routes, including Berlin, have been rebolted.

Wye Valley

■ *LOCATION* • Shorn Cliff, up the opposite hillside, and visible from the A446 Chepstow to Monmouth road just before the village of Tintern. GO Wall, at Wintour's Leap, which lies between the village of Woodcroft and the River Wye, two miles north of Chepstow.

■ *ROUTES* • The Laughing Cavaliers (HVS 5a), No Musketeers Direct (E1 5c), Kangaroo Wall (E2 6a), Vulture Squadron (E4 5c).

■ *FIRST ASCENTS* • The Laughing Cavaliers, No Musketeers Direct – Gary Gibson, Matt Ward (1984); Kangaroo Wall – Fred Bennett, Paul Lennard (1966), first free ascent probably Chris King (1978); Vulture Squadron – Arnis Strapcans, Chris King (1978).

■ *CONSIDERATIONS* • Shorn Cliff involves a 25 minute walk-in. There are access problems at the top of GO Wall: do not cross the land immediately behind the cliff, but abseil from one of 3 clearly sound abseil stations placed atop the main exits.

■ *GUIDEBOOK* • *Wye Valley*, ed. John Willson, Matt Ward et al. (Cordee, 1987). A new guide is rumoured for 1995.

CLIMBERS LOVE to talk about the horrors as well as the delights. Secretly, we all like the odd day when nothing goes right, when blocks crash on the ground at least five feet away, when three star routes turn out to be rubbish, when HVS routes are at least E2, and when we fail miserably to achieve any performance we can be proud of. It is not surprising, therefore, that when two or three climbers are gathered together, the mud tends to fly, and if they happen to have had bad days independently at the same crag, then the reputation of that place is soon cast in brimstone, and the direful tales become even more embellished at each airing.

Something like this has happened to the Wye Valley. The reasoning has probably gone like this: new guidebook to Wye Valley comes out; inquisitive climbers (all three of them) buy new guidebook; each visits Wye Valley and has a terrible time; accidentally, they meet in a hut in the Dolomites later in the year; after lengthy discussions, helped by too much wine, all agree Wye Valley to be dreadful; pleased that their own opinion agrees with other people's, they embark on a vicious all-out campaign to smear the Wye Valley in general, out of spite at spending money on new guidebook; new guidebook to somewhere else comes out ...

I mention this because people whose opinion I respect keep slating the place, even if they haven't been there! Many of those who have made the effort have been put off by bad experiences, and now believe the opinions circulating. Perhaps you are expecting me to say all this is nonsense, because the Wye Valley is in fact one of the best climbing areas in the country. Well, I am not. The Wye Valley is, I believe, a vastly underrated area, with some superb routes; but it is also an area with some really poor climbs, with whole buttresses that should be ignored. In short, I think it is an area that visitors need to approach with caution, with good directions, and with an open mind.

There are essentially five main crags: Wintour's Leap, Ban-y-Gor, Shorn Cliff, Symonds Yat and Wyndcliffe. Each has something different to offer, though for the visitor both Symonds Yat and Wyndcliffe are not really very safe bets. Ban-y-Gor is well worth a visit if you are in the company of a knowledgeable insider, but unless you are desperate to get lost in wild jungle, probably best left alone otherwise. The other two have a great deal to offer the travelling climber as a stop-off point, as well as the more adventurous daytripper. Both are close to climbing areas in Avon and in south-east Wales, so even a weekend can be salvaged if you really can't find anything to get excited about.

Shorn Cliff is about short routes at a generally amenable angle. It is about Sunday afternoons and pub lunches, about walking the dog, about tranquillity. The crag catches all the afternoon sun, and the best routes tend to be in the VS to E1 band, so it is ideal for lazy summer days when you don't really feel up to much. It is in a very picturesque setting, poking out of the trees overlooking the ruins of Tintern Abbey, and the same mellow atmosphere that caused Wordsworth to reflect on the meaning of life is still here. Walking up to the crag, through the forest, takes a leisurely 25 minutes, and is too pleasant to rush. The crag is quite long, with about 150 routes to try, and between 30 and 100 feet high. The rock is generally a sound natural limestone that is recognizable as such to Northerners, and it doesn't take much getting used to. Because of the canopy of trees beneath most of the crag, it is generally less pleasant after heavy rain and occasionally during the winter.

Although there are many good routes here, and certainly many that will repay the effort of visiting on a lazy day, the two outstanding routes on the crag are both on the same section, the Great Central Cave area. This is just under half-way along the crag, and easily recognized by the cave at its foot, formed by a huge leaning block. The Laughing Cavaliers (a superb HVS 5a) takes a line up the impeccable slab some 15 feet right of the cave, at a shallow groove in the wall. This is actually much easier than it looks, with adequate if not generous protection. As the groove merges into the upper slab, the climbing gets easier, with some balancy moves past a thread and good wire slots. From a second (*in situ*) thread, a tricky sequence of now steeper moves eventually leads up and left on to a big flake, and a couple of quite strenuous pulls on this bring the top within sight. A short scramble up to some stout trees rounds off the route. As for most of the crag, an abseil descent is recommended.

The other classic route here, No Musketeers Direct, climbs the wall and slab just right, with climbing that is both more technical and more strenuous, but very similar. Starting five feet right of the shallow groove of the first route, this E1 5c climbs fairly easily past an *in situ* thread on the lower wall, directly to a point just right of the upper thread on Laughing Cavaliers, before tackling the bulging wall above. An undercut flake marks the start of the difficulties and, although short, they are very sharp. Poor layaways need to be matched by positive pulls, and careful footwork is essential; fortunately, excellent wires up and right make this a good place to lunge if strength fails. Once above the bulge, a short scramble up left leads to good trees. A superb little boulder problem on top of a pleasant wall and slab round off an excellent outing.

In complete contrast to the laid-back atmosphere of Shorn Cliff, the Great Overhanging Wall at Wintour's Leap – or GO Wall as it has become known – is a crag with almost mountaineering appeal. Its huge size – 300 feet high and over 200 feet wide – is more striking from a distance than close up, but the immense roofs that split the central section of the cliff only assume correct proportions when you are directly beneath – or above – them. Initially the preserve of some spectacular aid routes, these roofs now give a series of dramatic free climbs, with sensational exposure. For anybody who revels in the challenge of long, demanding climbs, GO Wall is an exceptional venue. If the same climber enjoys the exposure that climbing above large overhangs high above the ground can give, then GO Wall becomes an essential venue.

Approaching from the Woodcroft Quarry, GO Wall is very obvious: the central band of overhangs being clearly visible from the path into Quarry floor. These huge roofs, level with the Quarry floor, are over 140

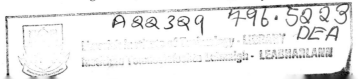

feet above the valley floor. GO Wall consists of three distinct vertical and horizontal sections. The horizontals are particularly conspicuous, being the ledge systems either side of the big overhangs at mid-height, and the obvious tree-filled Upper Terrace.

The left-hand section is bounded on the right by the obvious groove of King Kong, a classic HVS expedition, with a tough 5b crux at 15 feet that often stops parties from enjoying the 4c/5a climbing above. This section is characterized by small overhangs set in an otherwise featureless vertical wall. There are some short modern desperates at the foot of this wall: Eva Brawn and the Lurking Sear being typical sport routes and among the hardest routes in the area. Longer routes go in one or two pitches, through a cheesy band of rock, to a ledge system at half height and then steeply in a further pitch or two to the upper terrace, from where short pitches lead more easily to the top. Kaiser Wall and Blitzkrieg on this section are both excellent adverts for the crag that thoroughly deserve to become popular.

The central section is dominated by the great roofs at half height, and has more striking features. The groove lines taken by King Kong, Kangaroo Wall, Hyena Cage and The Jackal dominate the eye, although the mind will be stunned by the improbable ground taken by climbs like Feline and Dinosaur Heaven. Surprisingly, it is the wandering Vulture Squadron which provides the most outstanding experience on the wall. The central section ends at the right edge of the lower wall, where the scree slope runs down from the Woodcroft Quarry (with the right end of the big roofs and the Pedestal above).

The right-hand section is altogether more friendly, not least for starting in the sun from the ledge system gained easily from the Woodcroft Quarry floor. The Pedestal, an obvious square block at the end of this ledge system, is also the starting-point for a number of the routes that tackle the right-hand part of the central roofs without climbing the lower – more broken rock below. Directly above the ledges, short but often gymnastic pitches, like the accessible Never Say Goodbye and The Isle of Dogs, lead to abseil points or the Upper Terrace, and the pitches above the Upper Terrace are often ignored. The Pedestal area is also the starting-point for a number of interesting traverses, including The Umbrella Girdle (an ever-dry route just beneath the big roofs) and at a higher level, The Burning Giraffe, one of the best HVS routes on the crag.

On a first visit, be warned: climbing here is an acquired taste! Many parties end up facing benightment in the winter, as even the easier routes are quite draining in their length and situation. Having been forced to abseil off King Kong one January in my youth, and having subsequently never returned, I was very reluctant to give the place a second chance, until the summer of 1987. That was an incredibly wet year in the Peak District, and whenever I ventured further afield, I suffered the same fate. I arranged to climb with a friend who had recently moved to the Bristol area, and we found ourselves at Wintour's Leap. The sun shone there. I went home; it rained. Invited to return the following weekend, I was amazed to find the sun still shining, as it had done for the whole of that week. It turned out that the Bristol area had had a summer of virtually no rain. Weekend after weekend, I drove south in search of the sun and was rewarded beyond my dreams. I soon came to like Wintour's Leap. Despite (or because of) the awful routes, I always found something to do that seemed really good. Once I had got on to the bigger routes on GO Wall, I was completely hooked.

Kangaroo Wall (E2) is a good introduction to the delights of GO Wall. Only the second route to be climbed on GO Wall, it was the first 'XS' at Wintour's Leap. In terms of length and variety, it is a classic climb, crying out for a party of three with sandwiches and a flask. It begins about 30 feet right of the distinct groove of King Kong, at an obvious roofed corner. The first pitch requires the mature, thinking climber. The groove is climbed to a hard but very safe move out right below the roof. There is an easy way and a hard way, but it should be no more than 5c. Above, a prominent flake crack leads steeply, but with little technique to a good stance.

The next pitch should sort out the anorexic young hothead. Steep moves on small holds past a few bits of rotting gear lead to an overhang (and a very old peg that has seen a great deal of use!). A very hard move (6a) should gain a poor break and a thread, and some quick shuffling right in this leads to better holds, a chimney and eventually a cave stance. Traditionally 5c, this move is still aided by most parties. Above, the largest and most traditional member of the party should assume the lead. A chimney leads up and out on to the face in a superbly exposed position. Easier climbing then leads to the Upper Terrace. Any pitch from here gains the top, and a well-earned rest.

Kangaroo Wall lets you take a closer look at the roofs, but you don't really experience them. To do so, you need to take one of the other routes, the best of which is Vulture Squadron, an audacious expedition taking in some of the best 'moments' on the wall. Traditionally graded E3, few people feel they can be objective enough after an ascent to be accurate, and certainly the number of failures suggests an E4 attitude is adopted. The route begins up King Kong, climbing the whole of that route's first pitch to the terrace. Although long, the start is the only hard bit, and this only forms a warm up for what is to come. From the terrace you climb up about ten feet to the first horizontal break and then start traversing right. Various combinations of hand traversing, heel hooking and grovelling work, and you soon reach the belay in the chimney on Kangaroo Wall. The next pitch is only 50 feet, but covers some ground. Continue the traverse in the same line; the break is an awkward width, and stomachs, fists and feet can all be jammed in at various points. The problem is that the wall below you has slowly started to disappear, and by the time you reach the belay, an unmissable combination of pegs and tape (which you can back up with nuts) you are in a very exposed position.

By this stage the commitment is huge: 45-metre ropes only just reach the ground, should you be prepared to abseil from the belay, and, despite the lowly 5b climbing that has got you here, you are surrounded by 6a-plus territory. The next wall is the crux, and to make it interesting it is both difficult and bold! Small finger pockets and shallow breaks lead strenuously to a thin crack, and easier climbing to the traverse line of The Burning Giraffe, and a rest. More bold climbing, though slightly easier now, leads to the Upper Terrace and huge breaths of relief. It must have proved a thrilling experience for someone with only a few E3s under their belt!

Wintour's Leap is very popular with local climbers and often the broken sections well left of GO Wall are busy with groups of beginners, but you rarely find another party on the central bit of GO Wall. Next time you are passing by, give it a try.

WEST COUNTRY

Avon

- ■ **LOCATION** • Suspension Bridge Buttress, the Unknown Area/Upper Wall and The Sea Walls, Avon. The latter two areas form the first end of the stretch of cliffs above the A4, known locally as the Portway, as it enters Bristol from the M5, with Suspension Bridge Buttress located directly beneath the Clifton suspension bridge at the far end.

- ■ **ROUTES** • Limbo (HVS 5b), Yellow Edge (E3 5b/c), Arms Race (E4 5c), Edgemaster (E5 6b).

- ■ **FIRST ASCENTS** • Limbo – Ed Drummond, W. Hill (1966); Yellow Edge – Terry Gloag, P. Johnson (1972); Arms Race – Steve Monks (1979); Edgemaster – Martin Crocker (1985).

- ■ **CONSIDERATIONS** • The police are very quick to spot cars parked on the road, besides which the speed of the traffic makes this frightening. There is normally space below the Sea Walls end, with a pair of small off-road spots near the canopy beneath the bridge.

- ■ **GUIDEBOOKS** • *Avon and Cheddar* (Climbers' Club, 1992); *South West Climbs* by P. Littlejohn (Diadem, 2nd edn 1991).

THE BEST THING about the Avon Gorge is that it boasts such a diversity of climbing. Noisy it might be, beautiful it isn't, but it definitely has soul!

The two collections of photographic essays that were so inspirational in the late 1970s and 1980s, *Hard Rock* and *Extreme Rock*, did a great service to the local climbing community in Bristol. Tales came back from visiting climbers of rock polished like glass, of poor pegs serving as crucial runners, or even belays, and a good share of fear compulsory on each climb. Any visiting climbers with only the selection from Pat Littlejohn's first guidebook to use – for the Avon guidebook itself was a rarity even in Bristol – were no better served. The rock at Avon seems particularly easy to polish, and the fact that many of these climbs were actually quite old, even if originally climbed with aid, meant that many of them were unpleasant to nervous newcomers. Add to this a fair amount of parochial undergrading, and the picture of Avon as the crag every team stopped at, once, on their way to Cornwall is complete. But all the time there was another face, a face of rough features, to this giant city crag that holds some of the best climbs in the south-west, and for years the locals have had it all to themselves.

For newcomers to Avon, the best area to visit first is the Suspension Bridge Buttress. This fine crag of natural limestone is the only section of Avon that is similar to any of its counterparts elsewhere in the country. It has a good selection of steep and strenuous routes, all with plenty of incut holds and natural protection. Nearly all the routes on the buttress are worthwhile, sharing plenty of exposure and a quite unique atmosphere. It is not uncommon to be treated to a round of applause at the top of a route, even though the authorities forbid exiting on to the bridge itself. The canopy over the road makes a pleasant base at the foot of the cliff, despite the roar of the traffic reinforcing the feeling that you are actually in a city; and the bridge itself is an interesting feature.

My personal favourite here is Limbo, a good steep HVS that has some of the best pockets imaginable. It is also a good route on which to come to terms with the added ingredient to Avon limestone, a council-placed rock anchor. These enormous bolts provide interesting holds and even crucial runners on a number of Avon routes, and they are one of the more unusual features of this city crag.

Limbo is essentially a wall climb, although it attempts to follow a shallow groove where a line of pockets runs up the buttress. The holds are always good and the protection is as good as you could want, with plentiful opportunities for solid natural protection. In places, the climbing gets steep though, and a confident approach will save strength. If the pocket line is followed in its entirety, the route is about E1 5b, but an obvious detour out to the left of a rising crack, followed by some moves up and right, misses out the hardest section at HVS, though still 5b. The second pitch is the groove above, finishing leftwards at the break. At the top of the route you can scramble down to an unusual abseil point on top of the left arête of the buttress.

In complete contrast to the comforting nature of the rock and protection on Suspension Bridge Buttress, the Exploding Galaxy Wall lies at the other end of the gorge. Rising the full height of the gorge, this impressive wall offers sensationally positioned top pitches, on excellent rock, although some of the lower pitches require a grin-and-bear-it approach. For years the wall had a reputation for poor rock, and there are sections where this is still justified. A cheesy band of rock runs across the wall at

climbers could pose to tourists is therefore plain to see: imagine dropping a Friend Two from the finishing crack of Coronation Street, 370 feet up, on to the windscreen of a Ford Fiesta in the car park below! Replace the Friend with a brick-sized rock, and add a family, sat on the bank in front of the car, and the possible consequences become all too obvious. In addition, many of the cliffs also harbour rare flowers and the whole area is a designated SSSI. Consequently, there is a restriction that climbing should only take place between the start of October and the end of March (or Easter, should that fall early) on the south side of the gorge, and between October and February on the north side.

This means climbing at Cheddar is usually a cold affair, but that's not always the case: the sun does touch some of the cliffs, and the climate here is mild. It is certainly possible to keep warm with a bit of careful planning and a flask of coffee, even in January. The access restrictions may be prohibitive, but there are bonuses; many of the newer short routes have lower-off points *in situ* to prevent climbers damaging the clifftop flora, so you can enjoy the convenience of sport climbing, and a quick return to that duvet jacket, with an environmentally clean conscience.

The nature of some of the crags is more problematical. Even the biggest Cheddar fan will admit that the gorge is not without an unusually large share of loose rock and vegetation. Almost everybody I know who has climbed at Cheddar can tell you about some massive block that seemed held in place by a spider's thread, waiting to flatten some unsuspecting climber below. Many who have climbed there go further and tell you of blocks that were casually knocked off belay ledges, only to trundle with the accuracy of a guided missile into the path of a passing car. One belaying partner of mine vividly remembers the time we were pointed at a supposedly three-star classic, resulting in me pulling off a cement bag sized flake which shaved his chin and legs before nearly taking out a car in the road below. Be warned, there is a loose rock problem here!

But, again, it is a manageable one. Clearly, the biggest danger is to passing tourists, on foot or in a car, and the angle of the slopes is such that rock dislodged from anywhere seems to end up on the road. The recent cleaning of ivy and foliage from some of the upper tiers has made this problem worse: walk around the base of the Zawn or the Amphitheatre and you stand a good chance of dislodging something. There is an increasing amount of wire-mesh netting to catch the odd missile, but it is still a frightening situation. As there really are some giant trundles in the wings, it is fairly important to restrict your off-piste exploring to the times when no tourists will be about. On a serious note, it is worth stating that so far, despite a number of close calls, particularly with cars, climbers have not caused any major accidents; sadly, though, there has been at least one death attributed to falling rock and it can not be stressed too much that climbers need to exhibit a great deal of care in some places. The sort of third-party liability insurance that the BMC provides is a sensible prerequisite for climbing here.

The loose rock on the cliffs themselves is a surmountable problem: a combination of traffic (climbers not cars) and a judicious star system should mean that at least some routes end up clean and safe. The 1992 guidebook certainly addresses the issue of star ratings, with a sensible attempt to steer climbers at the more solid and clean routes. Unfortunately, this in itself will not be enough, partially because of the tenacious ivy that keeps working away at covering up and destroying the climbs. With no climbing during the summer months, battle has to recommence each October against the ivy which has had six months to regroup and push forward. The owners of the two sides of the gorge, the National Trust and Longleat Estates, have both indulged in massive ivy and scrub clearances recently, but the ivy still poses an active threat. The message is that climbs need to be picked carefully to avoid the hazards of loose rock and excessive vegetation, and to take account of the prevailing weather conditions.

Having said that, it is still possible to state unequivocally that Cheddar is home to some of the best climbing in the south, and certainly has some of the most dramatically positioned routes in England. It is a brave climber who can look up at the leaning Sunset Buttress without some trepidation, and the dark and foreboding look of High Rock must make all parties that stand at its feet, uncoiling ropes for one of the long routes, question themselves slightly. Consequently, it is very important to get the right introduction to the gorge. If your first outing is on one of the less good routes, loose or dirty (or both) it will be difficult to learn to love the place!

For these reasons once you have ceremoniously ticked off Coronation Street – which has now been climbed in virtually every style imaginable – Ahimsa on Acid Rock makes a good starting-point. Relatively short, enjoying some late afternoon and evening sun, and being on generally excellent rock, Ahimsa is one of the very best routes in the gorge. Park on the left hand side of the hill as you come out of Cheddar village, just opposite Coronation Street. This makes it much less likely that your car will be hit by rock! Acid Rock is just to the right of High Rock, and almost at right angles to the sunless wall of Coronation Street. An easy scramble from the car-park directly beneath the cliff quickly leads up to its base, and a comfortable base camp, from which it should be possible to avoid trundling rocks. The main face of Acid Rock is to the left of the prominent series of chimneys, and Ahimsa starts about 20 feet left of the chimneys, at a short groove.

The start is quite tricky and feels surprisingly bold, but the rock on the hard moves is reassuringly good, and the sense of exposure is small, so most E3 leaders will cope quite happily. Climb the groove and pull through the bulge with confidence into a further groove. Easier climbing lands you eventually on a reasonable ledge, below the second, crux, pitch. This begins up the main corner above, and then breaks out rightwards at a ledge on to the pocketed wall, heading for the obvious groove. Once gained, it gives superb and quite technical climbing, with plenty of fingery little holds and bridging moves past many fiddly but good wires to a small bulge and a peg runner. Step left and press on into the continuation groove, until it seems there is nowhere left to go. Look right and swing across to a projecting ledge, which is awkward to get on to, and thence up to the top. In all, this is an immaculate pitch, safe and full of intricate climbing; all the better enjoyed in the afternoon sunshine. It is possible to abseil back down, but a short walk downhill joins the main Coronation Street descent through some trees and down a polished gully.

If Ahimsa has gone well, then you should definitely head for Crow. An altogether different proposition, this famous climb packs plenty of variety into its 400-foot length, and it builds up to a thrilling finale on the head-wall left of Coronation Street. Low in the E3 and 5c grades, it is nevertheless a route not to underestimate. Given the likelihood of benightment by a slow party starting late, it is also not a route on which to join a queue, even though that is unlikely. Most teams take about four hours in good conditions. Take a torch if you are unsure, as the descent has some nasty steps in it in the dark.

Crow free climbs the lower two-thirds of West Route, beginning up a blatant roof-capped groove. The first pitch is a fun E2 5b in its own right, with exciting though relatively easy moves through the roof and some reasonable *in situ* gear to speed things up. The next pitch involves a bit of 'mixed' (rock and veg in variable proportions), but it is no harder than 5a and adequately protected. Above, the fun really starts. Climb the ivy to a grassy mantelshelf, and then easily to a higher ledge. Now stretch right into a good crack, and climb this strenuously until good flakes lead left-wards to an exposed belay. Suddenly you realize where you are, 250 feet above the road, and the wall above bulges. Up and left, the groove and roof taken by West Route continues to the top, but only at a very stiff E5 6a. Crow is forced 15 feet left to the slight weakness in the bulging wall, where flared cracks forge a line upwards. These are followed with sensational exposure, and by the time the crevasse belay below the final pitch is reached, most leaders will have had their money's worth. There is still a pitch to go though, 70 feet to keep a steady hand on before you can lie on the perfectly cropped turf and assure yourself that you are back in the land of the horizontal. If the exposure didn't get to you, walk over right-wards, facing out, to the rocky platform on the very edge of High Rock and imagine what it must be like for the BASE jumpers to look over that edge before taking the plunge.

High Rock is spectacular, and Crow really is superb, but Cheddar holds even more impressive walls further up the gorge. The monolithic block that forms Sunset Buttress seems to defy gravity, overhanging its base by as much as its width. Very obvious when looking up the gorge from Coronation Street, Sunset Buttress is another crag that gets plenty of afternoon and evening sun, and the deep groove-lines that provide some of the classic routes here are well highlighted by the autumnal sunsets. Home to no less than 12 routes of E5 and above, the undoubted plums are the two main groove-lines, the tapering left-hand line of Bird of Paradise (E6) and the slightly easier main central groove of Paradise Lost. Although the main crag is only some 130 feet high, it is perched in the air with its base a similar height above the road, which, combined with the ridiculous angle of the rock, gives the upper pitches a phenomenal sense of exposure.

Access to the ledge system that runs along the base of the buttress can be made by one of two ways. The approach described in the guidebook involves climbing up from the horseshoe bend and scrabbling through ivy on a fairly obvious line. Although probably the best approach on a first visit, there is much more fun to be had by coming in from above. This will either give you acclimatization time or frighten you senseless, depending on how well you judge the abseil route. The top of the buttress (a pleasant flat picnic spot completely at odds with the rock below) is easily reached from the main clifftop path, which, in turn, is best reached by scrambling up Shoot Gully, an obvious rake that cuts back up the hillside just before the road starts to level out. The aim is to abseil down the crest of the buttress; if done well, a single rope reaches from the good belays at the top to the ledge at the bottom. Put a knot in the rope though, and keep bouncing!

Paradise Lost must be as good a route as any here, although many of the harder additions look superb. It has two contrasting pitches, both well protected by a mixture of traditional gear and rotting aid relics. The first pitch has a series of desperately powerful moves with good rests in between, with a particularly strenuous sequence to get established above the second, bigger roof. Smearing footholds and undercutting frantically, you must be able to apply high-standard, limestone bouldering moves up here in the air. Above, the immaculate groove steps up leftwards, and this pitch is just sustained. Nowhere desperate, there are no real rests either, and the exposure is eating at your will-power all the time. The *in situ* gear is old but plentiful, and has been well tested. There are plans to replace the gear with modern bolts eventually, which, if judiciously placed, could make this a really thrilling pitch.

If even this can't get your adrenalin going, then head back towards the top of Shoot Gully from the top of Sunset Buttress, and pause for a moment to look at the Spacehunter Wall. How can a route, claimed by its creator, Martin Crocker, to be one of the finest routes in the area, still not have had a second ascent after ten years? Spacehunter certainly looks brilliant, and at E6 it should have seen many attempts; but it remains virtually ignored, a testament to Cheddar's latter-day guardian, and it will surely remain so until the rest of the country wakes up to what a wealth of climbing it is missing out on here.

Cheddar has always had the potential to be one of the finest venues in the country, and with a combination of increasing popularity and an absolute adherence to the access requirements, it may yet prove to be so. Gone are the summer days when you could set off up Crow or

Coronation Street at four in the morning; any action now that endangers climbing at Cheddar would be selfish in the extreme, as the access negotiations have been difficult, to say the least. It can be fun there in the winter, particularly in October, so take a flask, dig out your Helly Hansen trousers and enjoy!

DEVON AND CORNWALL

Lower Sharpnose Point

- **LOCATION** • Lower Sharpnose Point, four miles north of Bude, beneath a field full of giant white dishes and antennae that form an Early Warning Station.

- **ROUTES** • Lunakhod (HVS 5a), Out of the Blue (E2/3 5b), Fay (E4/5 6a).

- **FIRST ASCENTS** • Lunakhod – Keith Darbyshire, Pat Littlejohn (1971); Out of the Blue – Keith Marsden (1980); Fay – Pat Littlejohn (1986).

- **CONSIDERATIONS** • Quick drying and often sheltered from the wind, with a good helping of the sun. All routes are affected by the tide to some degree, and it is not always easy to escape from the foot of the crag once cut off by the sea.

- **GUIDEBOOKS** • North Devon and Cornwall by Iain Peters (Climbers' Club 1988); South West Climbs by P. Littlejohn (Diadem, 2nd ed. 1991).

MANY CLIMBERS know the delights that climbing at Baggy Point can bring, and most weekends will find a number of teams busy eroding the precarious path down to the Promontory or Long Rock Slab. Yet only a few miles further down the coast is an enormous wealth of rocky coastline, whose cliffs are normally deserted. The Culm coast of North Devon is an exciting climbing area. Stretching from Clovelly down to Bude, it is an exceptionally peaceful venue. The combination of an excellent campsite and pub in the village of Hartland, with opportunities for coastal walks (the unusual coastal scenery and bizarre rock formations are worth a visit in themselves) and watersports make it a very pleasant place to be.

My first visit to the Culm coast was inspired by a fanatical desire to get fit by walking the North Devon coastal path. Temporarily unable to climb through injury, I was keen however to explore some new areas and try out my first camera. Paul was keen to sample the climbing, so we set off from Coventry one Thursday morning with four days free and a hit list of a dozen routes that Paul would climb and I would capture on film, and 25 miles of walking. What I had not anticipated was the enormous ups and downs that the section north from Bude throws at you, and as I recall we only managed the four miles to Lower Sharpnose Point before we gave up the walking. While I had read about and seen some photos of the place, I was not really prepared for such an eccentric cliff. We abandoned our hit list 30 feet up one of the VSs on the south face of the South Fin, unable to come to terms with the rock.

Lower Sharpnose Point is one of the oddest climbing venues in the country. At first sight, it is difficult to work out why the three fins making up this excellent cliff are still standing. Three vertical walls, up to 140 feet high, each with two sides, stand parallel to each other and jut out from the mainland into the sea. Although each wall is over 50 feet wide, they are less than ten feet thick. It took me several visits to realize that the wall's thinness is actually good news, because it means that the rock must be of above average solidity for the Culm coast or they would have fallen down thousands of years ago. Also, from a more relaxed and accommodating viewpoint, it is good news because it has resulted in each wall warping slightly, which gives each of the six faces a slightly different character.

It is not just the cliff structure that is unique here: above the clifftop can be found huge white radar dishes, a surreal addition to the relatively unspoilt North Devon coastline. Considering the technology for picking up signals from all over the Atlantic (and beyond?) atop the cliff, it is amazing that it is perfectly possible to be cut off by the sea between any pair of the fins below and find yourself unable to escape and unlikely to be rescued!

On that first visit we abandoned the rock well before the tide threatened, and headed inland in search of food and drink, forgetting all thoughts of fitness that had inspired the trip. I have since taken many people there, and their first reaction is always the same: what is keeping those walls up? I have also witnessed a number of escape attempts up the steep slopes at the back of the fins, one of which involved a sheep as baggage, and my only comment is that it doesn't look much fun.

With this in mind, after finding your way round the aerials and down the grass slopes above the cliff, the first decision you need to make is whether to gear up at the top or take gear down to the foot of the climbs and risk having to haul it out or even abandon it to the sea. Most people opt for the latter, but it is certainly worth ensuring a light sack. Scrambling down to the right of the fins (as you look out to sea) quickly gains the rocky beach, and if the tide is out it is easy to move around the three fins and marvel at the geology of it all. Choosing where to climb is usually an easy decision: the north faces tending to be cold even in summer, and often retaining damp from the sea air, whereas the south faces get regular sunshine, and are climbable all year round.

However, to be fair, the north face of the North Fin is a very clean, attractive-looking wall, broken only by the obvious bottomless crack of Mascon towards the right-hand edge. Most routes on this face are hard but excellent, and all are committing; Mascon is neither hard nor excellent – just committing, as you can see right through the crack in the upper stages!

In contrast, the south face of the North Fin is a friendly place to climb. The obvious leftwards-rising break of The Smile (E1) divides the face, and the first route described takes the wall to the right of the start of this. Out of the Blue is only 85 feet long, but it feels a full rope length. Although graded E3 in the guide, a strong leader will probably find the 5b technical grade very reasonable, and there certainly are plenty of opportunities for protection. However, the route is steep, and the rock takes some getting used to. Good holds are often hidden, though they may be superbly incut; whereas what appears to be a flake from below, may prove to be a smooth scoop offering little assistance to groping fingers. Horizontal breaks provide the best protection, with Friends being invaluable: the breaks tend to be very crinkly, and the smaller nobbles are friable under pressure. Some care is needed setting up a belay at the top, but a willingness to jump over the other side shouldn't be necessary.

If all has gone well on Out of the Blue, then quickly get back down and round to the south face of the Middle Fin. This impressive sweep is home to some of the finest routes in North Devon – and some of the hardest. The most amenable is Fay, a line that climbs directly from the pointed block below the centre of the wall. Originally graded E5, many people have found it to be top-end E4, but there is plenty of potential to go wrong and create all sorts of difficulties near the top, so the E5 grade is justifiable. The route begins easily enough, with good holds and protection, following the obvious line slightly rightwards then leftwards with feet in the good crack until it ends. Above are two peg runners, and some fingery and committing moves are needed to pass these. There are positive small holds, but the climbing is sustained. Above the second peg bear slightly right to a thin crack. The rock is slightly flakier up here, and it is worth finding protection before committing yourself to the next few moves. Climb the thin, awkward crack to a break, swing left into a comfortable niche and you are nearly at the top. Even the last few feet have a bit of excitement about them though, and most leaders will find the top a pleasure to reach.

If you have timed your ascent well, you will have the chance to run round and get established on Lunakhod before the sea cuts it off. If, like me, you were too optimistic and spent too long on the top section of the route, your second will have wet feet and be very unhappy at having to climb the route carrying a rucksack full of shoes, duvets and flasks of coffee. The advantage of this tactic is that you will have to return another day, though, and there are plenty of other excellent routes to tackle besides Lunakhod.

Lunakhod was one of the routes on that original hit list of mine, but we were completely put off by its scale. It looked an essential climb even then, but on a number of subsequent visits I put it off, always finding something else that needed doing. When I finally got round to the route, finishing a perfect afternoon's climbing and looking for no more than a way out really, it was a surprise to find myself talking in terms of the best HVS in the area, if not in the south of England. Comparisons are not always helpful, but Lunakhod has the feel of a mountain route from the 1940s or 1950s – something like The Corner on Cloggy, with the odd hold that creaks slightly. It has also been compared favourably to Great North Road at Millstone Edge, which it certainly surpasses for line and position. It is a superb corner system running the full height of the crag, with a good crack at the back of it, and a few bulges towards the top to add a bit of exposure, always on good holds. A willingness to layback makes the route even better, and plenty of old-fashioned Stoppers and Hexes make the route safe and the positions enjoyable.

In fact, the comparison with mountain routes holds true for a number of climbs on the Culm coast. At cliffs like the sombre Blackchurch and Exmansworthy, it is advisable to wear helmets and even carry pitons on some routes. Nowhere is this more true than on the masterful Breakaway at Henna Cliff – 500 feet of steep shale, requiring ice screws, stakes, Terrordactyls (for cleaning holds!) and more. But the wall climbs at Lower Sharpnose are not the only exceptions, the coast has many friendly places like the short Screda Point (80 feet of exceptionally solid slab with a perfectly flat grass picnic spot above) or the truly beautiful Speke's Mill Mouth, with its steep slate-like wall boasting well-protected technical climbs next to a 70-foot waterfall.

On the Culm coast, every crag has its own character, and even on the same crag you can experience the geological equivalents of microclimates, moving from horror show to gem in a matter of feet. Most Lycra-clad hot shots, armed with microwires, will enjoy the classic slab climb of Sacré Coeur (E2 5c) on the solid sea-stack at Blackchurch; but those who venture on to the Verger (also E2 but only 5a) on the main wall behind will find a helmet and big dangling Hexes a great comfort, if not thick woollen plus-fours! At Exmansworthy, it is the approach that steals the limelight, involving multiple abseils (and jumaring out) and a great deal of common sense. In fact, Exmansworthy proves the transient nature of most Culm cliffs, and therefore the solidity of Lower Sharpnose, as portions of it subside to the beach at regular intervals. Further round the coast the aptly named Smoothlands provides bold open-slab climbing, and all the way down to the well-trodden and decaying Compass Point at Bude, it is possible to seek out the odd classic or nightmare, depending on your taste.

Despite that first visit ending in such dismal failure, four miles and one third of a route completed, the seeds of a passionate love affair with the Culm coast were sown, and every spring I look forward to another visit and the chance to explore a fresh piece of rock.

Lundy

- **LOCATION** • An island in the Bristol Channel, Lundy requires some organization to reach; details of boats and accommodation from the Landmark Trust, the owners, on 0628– 825925. The routes described are on cliffs called the Devil's Slide, the Diamond and the Devil's Limekiln.

- **ROUTES** • Satan's Slip (E1 5a, 320 ft); the Exorcist (E3 5b, 180 ft); Watching the Ocean (E6 6b, 270 ft).

- **FIRST ASCENTS** • Satan's Slip – L.P.Fatti, D.G. Ward (1970, with one bolt); the Exorcist – A.Strapcans, F.E.R. Cannings (1976); Watching the Ocean – G.Gibson, M.Ward (1985, with three bolts), P.Littlejohn, N.White (1989, without).

- **CONSIDERATIONS** • All three routes are unaffected by tide and relatively easy of access. On a first visit it is useful to have an old hand in the party to save time locating crags and descents.

- **GUIDEBOOKS** • *Lundy* by Gary Gibson (RNMC, 1985), a new guide is in preparation, due 1994/5; *South West Climbs* by P. Littlejohn (Diadem, 2nd ed. 1991).

ALTHOUGH ONLY 12 miles of sea separate Lundy from the mainland of Devon, climbing on the island feels as remote as you can get in Britain. A local community of no more than 30 people, supplemented by fewer than 100 visitors (many of whom have come for the peace and quiet rather than the climbing) makes the island feel spacious. The three boat trips per week to the island, cancelled in very poor weather, make the island both difficult to reach and occasionally impossible to leave! The descents to parts of the three miles of granite cliffs that line the west coast can turn even the shortest and easiest routes into memorable challenges, and the bigger cliffs harbour some of the finest routes in the south-west.

A trip to Lundy is one of the great climbing adventures. It begins with the sort of planning that normally is reserved for trips abroad: accommodation on the island is limited and needs to be booked in advance. It is possible to camp, although even camping spaces are limited and need to be reserved. A sturdy tent is an essential requirement; the wind generator that provides power on the island between 8 a.m. and 12 p.m. is rarely still! If staying for more than a long weekend, it is definitely preferable to get established in one of a number of curious dwellings available to the public. These range from the well-placed Old Light flats (an ex-lighthouse that despite being built on the highest point of the island is apparently of no value to ships at all), through the interesting Castle Keep cottage to the remote and tiny shanty of Tibbetts. The buildings each have a distinctive character and all have devotees, though it has to be said that Tibbetts is probably not a good bet on a first visit to the island.

The next question is how to get there? There are a number of options, although most people will find the choice a false one. Canoe is the cheapest, the technique being to leave Hartland at the right moment, aiming for Swansea and hoping that you judge the tide correctly. Many aspirants find themselves having to make serious adjustments to their course when they realize after a few hours that they are actually heading for Ireland; clearly only an option for the brave and experienced! The next cheapest, and somewhat safer, way is by private boat. Various fishing boats from Clovelly and nearby towns make use of the shelter of Lundy's Landing Bay, and it is sometimes possible either to hitch a lift or charter a boat. However beware of proverbial gift-horses: a friend was offered a free return trip on a Royal Marines landing craft – safe enough you would think. On an evening when the official Lundy boat, a large (if flat-bottomed) vessel, failed to sail, the enterprising Marines and guest duly set off. Three miles later there were no rucksacks remaining on the swamped deck of the craft, which then promptly developed engine trouble. Thankfully, defeat was admitted and the heaving mass turned back to Bideford. Only slightly improving weather allowed a rescue boat to pick up the bedraggled seafarers minutes before the landing craft went down barely a mile from safety! If, like me, you are a bit nervous at the thought of spending two hours on any size of boat, you can consider the helicopter option. Fast and exciting, this is probably the premier way to reach the island, but even here there is a dangerous precedent: Frank Cannings, an important pioneer on Lundy, had the misfortune to fall badly while descending to one of the cliffs; a helicopter rescue was arranged, and Cannings was duly picked up, only to face a worse situation when the helicopter rescuing him was forced to ditch in the sea on the way back!

However you travel, arriving on the island is too much of a relief to be the pleasure it ought to be, but it will not take you long to find your way around the shop/café/pub that is central to the island's social scene. More awkward is finding some of the many brilliant cliffs lining the west coast. As well as being over three miles long, the topology of the coastline can be confusing at first. The three routes chosen are all on clearly identifiable cliffs that are more accessible than some of the others, though that in itself does not make them superb routes. However, there are other factors that link them.

Firstly, all three are essentially slab climbs, of a type that is rare south of the Scottish border, being bold open routes requiring a committed approach. Secondly, they each were, and still are, good solutions to obvious blank bits of rock, being subtle natural lines and not eliminates by any means. Lastly, they feature in their history some of the main characters that have helped to shape the climbing style that makes places like Lundy so special.

Most climbers will associate Lundy with The Devil's Slide, as fine a piece of rock as any that can be seen in the UK. The original route – and one that almost all visitors to the island climb – takes a general line up the less steep lower half of the Slide before being forced on to the right edge as the angle increases, culminating in a traverse off left below the slightly impending head-wall. For many years it seemed that there could be no other routes on the Slide, for the rock offered little chance of any protection, and lacked any clear faults. However, in 1970, marooned on the island by storms, Paul Fatti took the momentous decision to place a bolt runner 90 feet up from the half height ledge system, in the centre of the Slide, and led the 140-foot pitch of Satan's Slip with the bolt as his only protection.

It was a bold effort, for bolts had seen little use as a tool for free climbing, and one that caused quite a stir. Climbing such a blank slab must have been considered by many other climbers, and it was surely the lack of possible protection that had held them back. Although a minimal use of artificial aids, Fatti's bolt could well have paved the way for others to be tempted on to blank faces with the reassurance of bolt protection. Ahead of its time, perhaps, the bolt was condemned (although used by many leaders) and when it finally evaporated into rusty dust its demise was mourned by none.

Nowadays, the climb is protectable to a degree, with small wires filling some of the tiny granite seams that were too shallow for the pitons that might have been accepted in Fatti's day. The lower pitches, to the half-height ledge, are normally soloed, being a gentle and easy introduction to the difficulties above. From the half-height ledge, a mixture of confidence and care leads briskly to the main difficulties as the slab steepens slightly. Many leaders will dismiss the pitch as trivial, but remove that chalk bag, leave those wires behind and make your second belay round the waist as you press your gymshoes on to the granite crystals ... can you not see why a bolt seemed such a good idea?

For all this, Satan's Slip was still a fair challenge without the bolt: the rock is as sound as you can get, escape is not impossible and the overall atmosphere surrounding the climb is friendly. Reverse some of these factors and you would think that a similarly unprotected climb would also justify a bolt or two. Such a route is The Exorcist, at the southern end of

have a spare rope tied to a small bluff of rock some 70 feet up from the top of the exit groove. The bluff usually has a small cairn on it, and the exit groove is fairly obvious at the cliff edge, slightly to the left (looking out). A timid party would do well to drop the rest of the rope over the edge, as the last 40 feet or so are effectively protectionless and, although straightforward, on less than perfect rock towards the top. Having done this, the state of the tide needs to be assessed carefully. It is possible to see the foot of Mercury from the south, and if the sea is low enough and calm enough there will be a small platform clearly visible at the base of the groove. Running left from here, you will see a series of ledges that eventually disappears round the arête. In calm seas, these are accessible at most stages of the tide. The choices are now obvious: a direct abseil on joined ropes to the foot of the corner, or a single rope length abseil just around that arête, followed by traversing the ledges to the foot of the corner.

Each approach has some merit; both have a fair share of excitement, with part of the abseil free, and some of the ledges very slippery, but on balance the sea-level approach is to be preferred, being less frightening and involving some good climbing in its own right. To approach at sea-level an abseil down the Baptist cliff is necessary. Descending the grass slopes in the area of the sewer pipe and then bearing right (facing out) will soon land you at the top of the Baptist cliff, and an obvious natural 'eye' gives a good anchor. The sloping platform you land on is tidal, but the landing-point should remain dry in calm seas. There are some impressive looking routes on this section of cliff, particularly at the right-hand side of the large sea-cave, where The Awakening and The Haze find their way through barriers of overhangs. My first route at Carn Gowla was the Baptist itself, graded E2 5c. It is one of those routes where the grade misinforms you as to the nature of the climbing. The lower section is, indeed, E2 5c, although stiff at that grade. As you get higher, the technical grade drops, but the E2 standard is maintained to the very last, with the final few feet being as gripping as any E2, despite the enormous holds and low angle reminiscent of a Diff! Subsequently, with more experience of the 'Gowla biscuit' rock formations, I might have enjoyed The Baptist, but as a first route it was not ideal!

Once down, you can pick your way south along the ledges, keeping a careful eye on the waves, beneath the huge expanse of the Sewage Pipe cliff. There are a handful of fair routes here too, including the superb Crystal Voyage, which gives a brilliant outing at a technically reasonable E1. Eventually, the ledges come to an end, and there is a smooth wall of some 70 feet to cross to reach the corner of Mercury. This is crossed by the Mercury Connection, an entertaining HVS that picks a way across the wall at a slightly higher level than the ledge system, before dropping down and round to the ledge beneath Mercury. The descending section is probably the hardest technically, so either the last climber across ought to be the most competent at this sort of thing, or the first should protect this section well!

Now established beneath the corner, the first thing that strikes you is that the crack in the back of the corner is rather large. A large Friend or some big Hexes may be a comfort, but I relied on a reckless approach: not mine, but my poorly sighted and unflappable partner's. Phil had obviously learned a great deal since those early days at places like Carn Kenidjack, however, because he had only gone a third of the way up the pitch before he refused to go on and insisted on descending. None of my cajoling – suggesting that a crack in which you had most of your body wedged had to be safe – could change his mind, and, given the lack of realistic alternative options, I duly took the lead. A brilliant pitch, 140-foot long and always interesting, awaited me: only 5a technically, but with some committing sections, as the walls either side of the crack are not normally helpful. Further, there is a commodious belay ledge at its top that makes you feel comfortable at being in the middle of this huge cliff. By the time Phil had joined me, I was talking about trying the wall to the right, The Andromeda Strain (a bold E4/5), and The Baptist experience had receded well into the background.

Above, the corner continues, with a subsidiary groove curving round to the right. This is the line to follow, and after a technical little section, which occasionally seeps, you are out on the slab and heading across to a faint pillar, with delightful moves on excellent rock. Once on the pillar, move up to two peg runners and a foot-ledge. This was originally a belay, but we had been advised to ignore it as the pegs looked dubious. It was a surprise, therefore, to find a bolt next to the pegs. Clearly, somebody had felt that its status as a belay needed enhancing, although putting bolts on a cliff that is so clearly an adventure playground seems completely out of place. This is the point at which The Andromeda Strain meets Mercury, and it is obvious how utterly different the former route would become with the addition of a few further bolts. It could be argued that the bolt makes a safe stance, and therefore no preplaced belay rope is needed at the top, as there will be enough free rope to reach adequate belays there. How long this stance would be safe though is debatable, and were my leader to fall from the very top, I, as second, would much rather be belayed back on the large ledge above pitch one with a number of good runners between us, than standing precariously at the bolt with a few poor runners between us. Predictably, the bolt has since gone.

Ignoring the belay option then, from the pegs some steep but relatively straightforward climbing leads up and then right to a break in the capping bulge. Here, a groove with large but dubious holds can be entered and followed carefully to the top. Looking down from the top gives you a good sense of the size of the route, with the sea seeming a long way below. It's not the sort of route you will do again and again, but, especially with the long approach, it is an immensely satisfying route that more than lives up to the line.

By complete contrast, the short, accessible pitches of Amnesty and The Cull near Lizard Point are routes that you will do again. Amnesty is an excellent little pitch, following an obvious line of weakness up the square block at Pen Olver, the last headland before Bass Point. Graded E4 5c, with warnings that a four Friend was necessary, in the *North Devon and Cornwall* guidebook, it must have put many people off, which is a pity. If you find yourself on the Lizard at any point, seek this little gem out.

The Cull is quite something else. It is hard to believe that routes of this quality, yet only barely E3, were still to be found in 1986. It is a flake/crack line that is all arms, with good protection for the strong, and plenty of adrenalin for the weak. The Cull deserves to become the new Yankee Doodle of Cornwall – the climb that everybody wants to do.

Dartmoor and Torquay

■ *LOCATION* • Low Man, a subsidiary tor next to Haytor, high up on Dartmoor, just off the B3387 Widecombe to Bovey Tracey road. Anstey's Cove and the Sanctuary Wall, Torquay. Take the Babbacombe road from Torquay harbour for about a mile, then the cove is signposted.

■ *ROUTES* • Aviation (E1 5b), Interrogation (E3 6a), Call to Arms (E4 5c), Empire of the Sun (E6 6b).

■ *FIRST ASCENTS* • Aviation – D. Bassett, H. Cornish (1961); Interrogation – F. Cannings, P. Badcock (1964) and Pat Littlejohn (1975), FFA Mick Fowler (1980); Call to Arms – Steve Monks, Ed Hart (1980), and Steve Lewis, John Godding (1983); Empire of the Sun – Nick White, P. Bull, A. Turner (1988).

■ *CONSIDERATIONS* • Low Man is very exposed to the vagaries of the weather. Anstey's Cove has developed into a fairly popular sport-climbing crag, with plenty of good weather all year round. The Sanctuary wall gets the sun from mid-morning, and is affected by rough seas.

■ *GUIDEBOOKS* • *South Devon and Dartmoor* by Pat Littlejohn and Pete O'Sullivan (Cordee, 1985); *South West Climbs* by P. Littlejohn (Diadem, 2nd ed. 1991); a new guide is due in 1994, edited by Nick White.

CLIMBERS FROM the Peak District are ridiculously proud of their jamming expertise, born out of contact with the rough gritstone of Stanage and the Roaches. A classic example of this was provided by a well-known Peak climber visiting Yosemite, who, on encountering a pair of climbers cleaning up their badly mauled hands in the washrooms, held up the unbroken skin on the backs of his hands and said, 'See that? Gritstone hands, they are,' smiled proudly and left them to it. Whether the first free ascensionists of the Salathé Wall were impressed by this or not, history does not record!

The first time I heard about Haytor, I detected that same pride: a friend had just called in on his way back from Cornwall, done one route which he had found very over-graded and pronounced that 'the routes are all easy there, they just can't jam those Devon yokels!' Despite this to whet my appetite, it was some years before I came to see for myself, and my first encounter resulted in numb fingers and toes as the clear rays of the September sun were no match for the icy wind beating across the moor. I was quite impressed with the wildness of the place, though, and resolved to return in warmer times.

It was some eight years later that the opportunity finally came round. An abortive and unnecessarily frightening trip to Ladram Bay, home of some of the most impressively unclimbable cliffs in the country, found Dave and myself retreating to ice creams at four o'clock in the afternoon on a perfect June day. Full of physical energy (though our nerves were somewhat tatty), a gentle route was needed, and Haytor seemed to fit the bill.

On arriving at the very large car-park that lies just down the slope from the crag, I was depressed to see that the isolation I had previously felt here was a rare and lucky moment. It was like watching ants at work. We ran up the slope nevertheless, adopting a pragmatic rather than aesthetic approach, and aiming just to do as much climbing as we could. Despite the huge number of people there, this approach worked well, and we quickly dispensed with a bagful of stars on Haytor itself, before moving across to Low Man. Unbelievably, this was deserted, with presumably none of the tourists interested in this lower summit. For climbers, however, Low Man is of much greater interest, being both higher and bolder in architecture than its neighbour.

Nearly all the routes here are excellent, but two of them have become much sought-after classics, and it is easy to see why. Both Aviation and Interrogation are superb routes, the former boasting a strong natural line and the latter tackling some very unlikely looking ground.

The ability to jam is not strictly necessary on either route, but it certainly makes the first 20 odd feet of Aviation a joy, and very easy, if you can relax on some sharp but very positive jams. The alternatives of lay-backing or swimming look very unappetizing, although they will no doubt provide more amusement for any onlookers! Above, a balancy traverse (surprisingly delicate after what has come before) leads rightwards to a good belay in a niche. A peg is *in situ*, but with care a number of good wires can be found to make a relaxing stance. Although hating grit-stone, and climbing chalk free as ever, Dave soon joined me on the stance and eyed the upper groove. This is an amazing feature, a runnel that leads steeply at first and then more gently on to the upper slabs. Barely pausing to grab some wires, he was off, and in no time the rope was tight and it was my turn. Having climbed together often enough to know that he would not pull the rope tight unless it was safe to climb, I set off, thoroughly enjoying the layaways and smeary footholds. The rope seemed to get taken in very quickly, and by the time I had reached the easy slabs at the top I was virtually running, but still the ropes stayed tight. As I rounded the huge dome I could see why as Dave was running too, across the grass; truly a dynamic belay! Quickly, without untying, we sprinted round to the foot of Interrogation. Now, I usually do use chalk, much to Dave's disgust, but as I reached into my rucksack to get the evil little bag, I heard a delighted little chuckle behind me.

'Is this what you are looking for?' said Dave. He held up my chalk bag.

I nodded and he threw it across to me. As I caught it, I knew what had happened. As we were gearing up to descend to Ladram Bay Dave had muttered something about needing a bag for his six-inch nails ... the chalk bag was full of nails, and completely empty of chalk.

Determined not to let him get away with this, I adopted a casual approach. 'No need for chalk in the evening any way,' I said, and looked up confidently at the smooth face. It appeared hard, with some very blank bits between good-looking breaks. There were pegs to go for, though, and it really wasn't that hot any more, so I carefully cleaned my boots and hands and set off. A tricky start to the first break, and a slightly downward-pointing peg. Then a tricky move on some poor layaways brings some better holds and an incipient crack into reach. From here it seemed easier, with mainly good holds, some excellent runners, wires and Friends and the odd peg (particularly useful on the perplexing moves left). By the time I was clawing the jugs up the steeper groove above, I was really enjoying myself. I swung left to belay, and settled down to enjoy the last of the sun. Things didn't go exactly to plan though, and Dave declined the second pitch, so once more I got ready for action, and headed across to the famous mantelshelf. After some indecision, I decided to go for a full-frontal attack, and executed the most desperate mantel I have ever done. After that the bold slabby wall above seemed very straightforward, and I was quickly descending the dome-like summit to the grass below. I found a suitable boulder to sit behind and took the rope in. Dave followed very promptly, declaring my mantelshelf completely unnecessary and carefully explaining his no-hands rockover without even noticing that I had untied from the ropes and had used no gear to belay on: or if he did, then he was playing the same game and didn't say. By now it was nearly dark, and a mad dash to the Double Locks in Exeter for superb food and beer, and a camping spot in the garden, rounded off a brilliant day.

As well as the beauty and sheer fun to be had on Dartmoor, South

Devon is also, in climbing terms, strongly associated with the sea-cliffs of Torbay. Here lies the venerable Berry Head, with its brooding sea-cave and stunning roof lines. The phenomenal Caveman, a first ascent of great audacity, has lost none of its difficulty for having been soloed by Dave Thomas. Indeed, I found that the constant interruption to my thoughts that Dave's exploit triggered made it very difficult to concentrate on the climbing (which is basically very obvious but very frightening). I kept thinking what would have happened if this or that hold had snapped, or trying to imagine how the hand traverse would feel with no gear and just the sea to catch me. The feeling was particularly strong because I had experienced it before, on a route on the Sanctuary Wall at Long Quarry Point, Call to Arms.

I can't really explain why Call to Arms took my imagination so strongly, but I became quite besotted with the route almost from the moment I first saw it. Sanctuary Wall is not a place for the faint hearted, but lured there by the quite poor Sacrosanct when climbing no harder than HVS, I was stunned by the ridiculous walls of rock to either side. The groove of Call to Arms struck me then as being the only feasible line, and when, some three days later, I found out that it had just been climbed for the first time, I was determined that one day I too would climb it.

Subsequent guidebooks described the route as three star, and only 5c (despite an overall E4 grade), and as I got better I kept on thinking about that wall. Although I visited Torbay fairly regularly, I never went round there, and by the Summer of 1991 I had almost forgotten what the wall looked like, until that is I read in *Mountain* about Dave Thomas's eventful solo of Call to Arms. Dave was well known by then for his soloing ability, and he had set out to solo the route – well within his capability – with Glenn Robbins taking photographs. Unfortunately, after about 80 feet Dave had what affects the rest of us very regularly when soloing, a complete grip, and he called for a top-rope. At this point, it is essential to appreciate that the Sanctuary Wall overhangs severely, and so any time spent holding on is precious time; some 20 minutes later, after what must have seemed eternity to Dave, a rope was lowered: but, inevitably, there it hung useless, 15 feet out from the now desperate climber. With no other options, Dave refocused his attention on to the climbing and managed to hold his shattered nerves and exhausted body together for long enough to make it to the belay, and then to safety down the easier (but still gripping to solo) first pitch of Incubus.

When the time finally came for Call to Arms, I was ready to be shocked by that solo, for I could remember the wall looking steep and forbidding. What I wasn't prepared for, though, was the climbing itself. I expected a steep romp on jugs: I assumed a certain amount of solidity otherwise nobody would have dreamt of soloing it. So up I went, a little nervous as there was a slight damp feel to some of the lower holds, but basically feeling strong and expecting success. The first hold that snapped frightened me a little, but I had some fair gear behind a sound flake, and although steep, I managed to absorb the weight on my other

Steve Bowker on Swordfish
(Alan Leary)

Previous page:
Abseil into Lost In Space
(Alan Leary)

Gary Gibson on Mother of Pearl
(Hazel Gibson)

Cliff Brown on Lunakhod
(Bill Birkett)

Steve Mayers on Fay
(Glen Robbins)

Dave Birkett on Satan's Slip
(Bill Birkett)

Opposite page:
Dave Birkett on Interrogation
(Bill Birkett)

Alan James on The Exorcist
(Paul Dearden)

Dave Birkett on Mercury
(Bill Birkett)

Opposite page:
Unknown climber on
Empire of the Sun
(Paul Twomey)

John Adams on Buccaneer
(Bill Birkett)

Luke Steer on Wombat
(Bill Birkett)

Wilf Williamson on
Angel Fingers
(Bill Birkett)

Martin Moran on
Greenford Road
(Keith Sharples)

Rob Knight on White Noise
(R.E. Wightman)

Above left: Dai Lampard on The Sun *(R.E. Wightman)*   *Above right:* Ashley Lewis on Warpath *(Alan Leary)*   *Below:* Mike Lynch on Ten Years After *(R.E. Wightman)*
Opposite page: Chris Hamper on The Golden Mile *(David B.A. Jones)*

Above left: Steve Monks on Paradise Lost *(David B.A. Jones)*   *Above right:* Phil Davidson on Cave Route Right Hand *(David B.A. Jones)*   *Below:* Steve Mayers on Specular Reflections, part of the first pitch of Wall of the Evening Light *(Ray Wood)*

Above left: Unknown climber on Pull My Daisy *(Dave Wilkinson)*   *Above right:* Sally Ingham on Ride the Wild Surf *(Alan Leary)*   *Below:* Nigel Smart on Clonus Left Hand *(Dave Wilkinson)*

Sally Ingham on Ride the Wild Surf
(*Alan Leary*)

Al Rouse on the first ascent
of Citizen's Edge
(*Ian Smith*)

Mike Lea on Tax Exile
(Kevin Eloury)

Following page:
Brian Rossiter on Mandarin
(Chris Craggs)

Andy Popp on
All Roads Lead to Rome
(Gary Gibson)

arm. Ten feet higher, the holds started getting smaller: I placed a poor
Rock 3 and contemplated pulling on a thin-looking flake. Being cautious
and worried about the wire, I decided to retreat a few moves to a bridging rest. I climbed down carefully and put my hand on to that flake with
all the good gear. The moment I started transferring my weight the
whole thing came off: rock, gear, me screaming – we were all in space.
Unbelievably, the Rock 3 had held. Thoughts of Dave Thomas soloing
this route came flooding into my terrified brain: what was he doing?

I descended and tried to psych up for another go. A couple of south-
west locals had arrived by now, and hearing Andy talk about how hard
and scary the upper bit of Call to Arms was did nothing to help my shattered confidence. I set off again, but this time I knew I was going to fail,
and after reaching my pathetic Rock, and clipping a peg out on the right
wall, I decided to end the torture and return another day. I was unusually happy to leave gear behind that day, and when I got back to the car I
felt as satisfied as I have ever done from climbing. I am still convinced
that Call to Arms must be one of the great adventures; but I haven't been
back yet.

In complete contrast, the steep walls at Anstey's Cove, from where
screams on the Sanctuary Wall can be heard all too clearly, are much
more forgiving. The angle at times is no less, although there are some
excellent slab routes too, but the inherent stability of the rock and the
sound fixed protection have inevitably resulted in a sport-climbing cru-
cible, with some of the hardest pitches in the south-west, and with some
astonishing projects yet to come to fruition. As a place, Anstey's Cove
leaves much to be desired: the stream of tourists descending to the little
beach, invariably moaning about the steps, and the incessant bleating
from the pleasure boats below make it a venue where you have to ignore
your surroundings and put the climbing first. This is more than compensated for by the ridiculously good weather that Torquay enjoys, often
making midsummer visits a very sweaty affair. Indeed, it is well worth
visiting late in the year, before any seepage appears and when the tem-
peratures are more moderate.

The first rock you see at Anstey's is a very steep wall, terminated by
the arête of The Mitre. For sheer unlikeliness at the grade of E4 6a, The
Mitre ought to be a great climb, but sadly neither the climbing nor the
positions live up to expectations, and it is the central line on the rearing
wall to the left that provides the classic of the crag. Empire of the Sun is
the epitome of the modern stamina route. Barely 6b for a move or two
low down, it is nevertheless steep and sustained at 5c or just above for
most of its length. Four bolts now mark the way, adequate protection
when you are strong, but seeming very spaced when not fit enough. The
climbing is nearly always obvious, always good, and the feeling of relief
as you lower back to the ground after a successful redpoint is very pleasant, if not very intense. I'm sure that climbing the big routes on the
Sanctuary Wall gives an even greater feeling, but sometimes you don't
want that sort of intensity.

SOUTHERN ENGLAND

Swanage

- **LOCATION** • The limestone cliffs at Swanage run westwards from Durlston Country Park, a mile south of the town of Swanage, on the Isle of Purbeck just south of Poole.

- **ROUTES** • Buccaneer (E2 5b), The Conger (E1 5c), Ocean Boulevard (E3 5b/c), The Mind Cathedral (E5/6 6a/b).

- **FIRST ASCENTS** • Buccaneer – Richard Crewe, K. Winkworth (1969), FFA Gordon Jenkin, R. Harrison (1978); The Conger – R. Crewe (1969), FFA R. Farrell (1979); Ocean Boulevard – K. Turner, N. Buckley, S. Bartlett (1979); The Mind Cathedral – Pete Oxley, S. Williams (1988).

- **CONSIDERATIONS** • The rock at Swanage is very variable in quality, and some care is needed at the foot of most of the cliffs, particularly near abseil lines. Only a rough sea affects these routes, though a low and calm tide is a comfort on The Mind Cathedral. Both The Conger and The Mind Cathedral suffer from seepage.

- **GUIDEBOOKS** • *Swanage* by G. Jenkin (Climbers' Club, 1986); *Swanage Supplement 89* by G. Jenkin, P. Oxley and N. Coe (Climbers' Club, 1989) – although much of this information can be found in the British Mountaineering Council's New Routes series from 1986–88; *South West Climbs* by P. Littlejohn (Diadem, 2nd ed. 1991).

SWANAGE TERRIFIES me. Most people have a crag that always intimidates them, or that they just can't get to like, and for me it is Swanage. It has all sorts of features in common with other sea-cliffs that I love, but there is some indescribable quality that guarantees I will always have a bad time there. I have tried to rationalize this. I am not a strong swimmer, and I am very frightened by the thought of ending up in the sea; yet the sea is much less of a problem at Swanage than at many of my favourite crags, and the chances of ending up in it are much lower, as there are only a few areas where you could get cut off by the incoming tide. I don't like abseiling; but I am quite happy to put up with it as a means to an end on all sorts of other cliffs, and, despite the steepness of the Swanage cliffs, the abseil descents are not particularly gripping. Protection is often good, and although there are some loose tops, these are rarely hard, and belays are usually good. Consequently, it is difficult to understand why I hate climbing at Swanage! I think it boils down to not liking rock which feels as if it might fall down on a whim: I don't dislike rock that feels snappy, because an element of skill and judgement comes into climbing it, but when you suddenly get the feeling that hundreds of tons of the overhangs you are about to pull round might just decide it is their turn, then I am unhappy.

I know, however, that Swanage is a brilliant place to climb, and I also know there are superb routes there. I ought to explain: I have no grounds whatsoever for doubting the integrity of the cliffs, it is just a feeling. I have only a few trivial experiences that might explain why I get this feeling, but the power of it to distract brain and body from the task in hand is often so great that I am forced to return to the ground and persuade someone else to climb. You know how it feels at the beginning of a year when you have done little real climbing for a while, and you are continually checking your knots and the buckle on your harness, and gripping the rock so hard that you get pumped after 20 feet on even the easiest of routes? The worst case of this I remember was one spring Bank Holiday in France, when I got to the point that I could not even second anything, because I was so worried about the lower off failing when I reached the top – this despite the lower off being formed from substantial bolts and chains, and the evidence of everybody else returning safely to the ground suggesting that I was wrong.

Sometimes I forget, and I leaf through a guidebook, or talk to friends, and think, 'Hey, I haven't been to Swanage for a while, I'd love to do that Lean Machine.' I'll arrange partners, head off down there on a Saturday morning, arrive in splendid sunshine, all excited and knowing that it's just been a bad choice of routes before that caused the problem and this time it will be OK. Then I'll run to the cliffs, abseil down without so much as a frown on my brow, find something to warm up on – 'This looks good, what grade is this then?' – and off we go. I get ten feet off the ground and I know I should have forgotten about the warm-up and just got on with it, but I get all determined. 'Come on, it's only HVS,' I say to myself, as I carefully pick myself up some rotting corner, grinding the salt into the rock with my clumsy feet, and starting to darken the rock with my sweaty hands. By the time I get two-thirds of the way up, I have got *that* feeling back. My stomach drops, as I nervously sink on to what is probably the best Rock 8 placement in the world, apart from the one a foot below (that would be even better if I hadn't jammed that Friend 1 in just below it). My mind assures me that the string of runners I have just placed are all perfect, but my body is braced for the jolts as each one rips. They don't, of course, and I reach the ground in one piece physically, though my soul is in pieces. So I never get round to Lean Machine, and although it is a brilliant-looking route, I somehow doubt that I ever will.

It was from this sort of day that I salvaged Ocean Boulevard, however, so I am confident in saying that this is a totally worthwhile pitch. Anything that can restore morale to the extent that this did – through a combination of big holds, excellent runners and interesting moves – must be a classic. I think another reason why I enjoyed Ocean Boulevard so much was that it felt easier than I expected, not requiring much mental involvement. Often when depression has set in, you can overestimate the difficulties, and I was pleasantly surprised. Even though it is dauntingly steep, there are good rests, particularly if your jamming technique is good, and the open nature of the wall, combined with the relatively low technical difficulty, allows you to be elegant, if you have the strength.

I might have been forgiven for feeling that I had beaten the Swanage curse after Ocean Boulevard, but it was not to be. As the foot of Lean Machine had become a bit damp by then, we decided to make our way back towards the car, and stop for a route in Boulder Ruckle East on the way. For some bizarre reason, I ended up on what turned out to be a grown-up version of the horror show of the morning, a route that sums up what I can't seem to come to terms with at Swanage – Buccaneer. I confidently predict that everybody else who has ever done this climb, and everybody in the future who will do it, would testify that it is a classic. It looks a classic: a giant corner that narrows to a roof, above which leans an excitingly positioned head-wall – what a line! For me, however, the gritty bottom corner (standard 4c) felt hard, and I was unhappy with both rock and runners. The prospect of the 5b pitch didn't appeal at all, and I deliberately took a stance about ten feet below the roof that would make anything other than leading through a nightmare. Andy arrived at the stance and seemed quite happy to carry on, so, thankful that my ordeal had nearly ended, I almost stopped looking at the six runners I was belayed to, and tried to enjoy the position. All went well for a few minutes; Andy disappeared round the roof and I began to relax completely – my earlier qualms about the solidity of the cliff starting to be enveloped in the sense of relief that one of us would soon be anchored to something firm at the top. Unfortunately, I had forgotten Andy's propensity for neglecting to place runners and then taking massive screamers. The sky went black; I was jerked violently upwards, ripping the very belays I had just started to trust, and I slammed into the underside of the roof. Andy was left spinning in space 20 feet beneath me. The panic soon subsided when I realized that there were at least three runners between us still in the rock, including one round the lip. It was difficult to unwind though, as my bare shoulder had grated against the rock, and my leg was bleeding. Andy, meanwhile, was laughing and whooping with delight. He could not sense my fear at all, so it would have been pointless to say 'Please don't fall off again' in a polite way. Whatever the exact words I employed, he didn't, and, what seemed ages later, I somehow clawed my way back to the horizontal and safety.

I have tried to overcome my problem with Swanage. I have sneaked up to it from the far end, making the surroundings unfamiliar, and pretending it was just another new crag. I have tried ignoring the warm-up and getting straight on to supposed classic routes that I knew nothing about. I had a particularly horrible day at Fisherman's Ledge, trying this; failing on The Ritz, due to feeling the huge block that forms the first big roof vibrate, I decided to try Freeborn Man. It looked solid and my sort of climbing, but unfortunately the scraps of paper that stood for our guidebook made no mention of the lack of protection. I was very lucky to escape a dunk in the sea, which is at least a good landing, and felt completely unable to do anything else all day. However, what we did do was explore, and this was my first look at The Mind Cathedral. It says a lot about Swanage that this route has failed to capture the imagination of the climbing public, being a quite staggering line for its grade. Certainly, it is not the most impressive roof in the country, but there is little similar that is both in the same grade and so accessible. It is a huge cave, with such an obvious line leading up to the roof and out to the lip, above which a short, easy-looking head-wall leads to the top. I spent a good hour or so eyeing up this route, wondering if I had the guts to come back another day and try it. The first section looked straightforward – a chimney leading through a bulge and out on to a suspended tooth. From there it just looked steep, although flakes seemed to line the roof itself. Odd loops of tat hung invitingly from the roof, making it look a possibility. I left thinking I would wait until I felt ready, and then come down just to do The Mind Cathedral.

As it happened, I was too excited to wait long, and having climbed E4s and E5s solidly in the Peak District for a few weeks to restore confidence, I returned. All I can say is that I am impressed by Pete Oxley's achievement. I reached the point where I had had enough after about four attempts. It is all there – the majority of holds being very good and the protection reassuring – but it is desperately strenuous, and in the end I just wasn't up to it. However, at last I had enjoyed something at Swanage, so I came out of the cave happy; so much so that I decided to end the trip by soloing The Conger. As the guidebook implied this was totally solid, and as I could see that the landing was deep water, with a vague memory that someone had told me that it was only the start that was hard, this seemed like a good idea.

Beware those moments in life when you ignore experience and act on impulse. I should have known that soloing at Swanage was not a good idea! Climbing unroped at a crag that always seems to get me scared witless! Not even pausing to contemplate what might happen, I duly set out. The Conger is a weird route, traversing out above the lip of a sea-cave, but only a few feet above the sea, until a bottomless chimney forces you up and out on to a short wall that leads to the top. I carefully picked my way across the base of the Freeborn Man wall, remembering that episode with a twisted sort of smile. The initial slab was streaked with water, and it did feel hard, but some good holds at its apex led round and on to the traverse proper.

All went well, and I was actually enjoying it, until I reached the base of the chimney. The chimney is tapered, narrow at the top and very wide at the bottom, and the side you are on is actually very steep, so that when you swing into the chimney you are immediately on an overhanging wall. I could see that I needed to swing round, pull up and get bridged as quickly as possible, but the bridging looked dauntingly wide, and the holds I needed to pull into the chimney were very greasy. I contemplated going back, but that didn't appeal much either, and jumping into the sea was out of the question. I agonized for ages, but eventually decided that the free fall into the sea if I came off would probably be better than jumping voluntarily, so, heart pounding, I swung round. The next few minutes were a blur. I remember shouting in the manner of a child whose mother has taken away its toy, and I may even have used the same vocabulary! I remember being uncomfortable at the top of the chimney but being hopelessly frightened at the thought of moving anything. I vaguely remember the surge of adrenalin in my already racing blood as I felt a hold move (which it probably didn't), and I remember feeling cold, despite the heat of the sun as I lay pinching myself at the top.

With a few years to smooth the memory I look back on The Conger with a mixture of horror and amusement. Every now and then I give Swanage another go, although I try to avoid anything remotely hard, and usually try to bring along a keen leader! The Mind Cathedral is apparently a touch harder now, but I would still like to try it again one day. I just hope I'm not there the day it all falls down.

Jersey

■ **LOCATION** • Various sea-cliffs around Grosnez Point, the north-western tip of Jersey. A car is useful but not essential, buses are common and locals are friendly. Cheap accommodation is limited out of season and needs prior booking in season; some campsites only allow mixed couples!

- **ROUTES** • Perihelion (HVS 5a, 130 ft); Citizen's Edge (E1 5c, 170 ft); Tax Exile (E5 6a, 210 ft).

- **FIRST ASCENTS** • Perihelion – A. Rouse, R. Haszko; Citizen's Edge – A. Rouse, J. Curran, R. Haszko; Tax Exile – A. Rouse, P. Burke; all Easter 1984.

- **CONSIDERATIONS** • In calm conditions all three routes are accessible at any state of the tide; Perihelion involves an abseil approach. Walk-in less than 15 minutes.

- **GUIDEBOOKS** • *Jersey and Guernsey* by I. Smith (Cordee, 1987); *Jersey Rock* written and published by Kevin Eloury (1993); *South West Climbs* by P. Littlejohn (Diadem, 2nd ed. 1991); *High 21* (August 1984) has an article by Jim Curran describing the first ascents of these routes.

THERE ARE few places described in this book which are so ideally suited to a family holiday as Jersey. Travelling there is easy to organize; flights are available from most airports and car hire is cheap, or you can take your own car and enjoy the nine-hour ferry journey from Poole. Once on the island it is difficult not to feel on holiday; street names are in French, *pâtisseries* sell *baguettes* and *pain chocolat*, a speed limit of 40 mph slows life down and the weather is invariably an improvement on what you have left behind. July and August bring thousands of holiday-makers to the gloriously sunny beaches, but if you are prepared to travel slightly out of season, you will find the island relatively quiet.

Jersey has everything: from small jumbles of boulders to impressive cliffs, tacky little corner shops to glitzy shopping areas, crazy golf crowds to wild and lonely coastal paths, Neolithic burial sites to relics of the Nazi occupation. Jersey provides most of the elements that climbers, sunseekers, travellers and holiday-makers all could wish for. On top of that, it is relatively cheap – there are few taxes levied on goods, so petrol, alcohol and many luxury items are substantially cheaper than on the mainland. If you wish to eat out, there is a full range of establishments, whose quality is nearly always outstanding.

The climbing on Jersey is concentrated into the few miles of coast that don't boast golden sand; particularly at Les Landes, near Grosnez Point in the north-west, Sorel Point on the north coast and La Cotte de Sainte Brelade on the south coast. Sorel Point provides short, interesting pitches on gabbro, and is well worth a visit on a lazy warm afternoon. La Cotte is the site of a prehistoric cave dwelling, and as it rises from a perfect beach it is also worth a visit at lowish tide, when an enjoyable amount of bouldering can be accompanied by sunbathing and swimming. There are some big routes here too, but generally they are less enjoyable than those at Grosnez.

Les Landes is a compact area, less than a mile of coast, covering about a dozen cliffs. The rock is a uniformly sound granite, a rich pink in colour when warmed by the evening sun. The sea is a factor with all routes here, the tidal range being particularly impressive; but if calm, it presents few problems. There is ample parking at Grosnez Point, just in front of a ruined castle, and the cliffs can all be reached easily and quickly. There is also plenty to interest non-climbers here, with the lighthouse at the tip of the point and a number of structures and artefacts from World War 2 littering the coast. There is a good chance that you will meet local climbers here too; there is an active core of very amiable enthusiasts who are out most weekends and holidays. It is common practice to leave a note on the dashboard indicating probable location if you are looking for other climbers.

One of the delights of Jersey is that, because of the holiday atmosphere, even the shortest routes can be enjoyed lazily: there are numerous routes in the 20- to 40-foot range, and some, like Open Heart Surgery (HVS 5a) at Rouge Nez, are excellent. Whole days can be spent mixing a mere handful of such routes with liberal doses of sunbathing, swimming and eating ice cream without any feelings of guilt. However, there are at least three routes that have both a substantial feel to them and deserve much wider recognition.

Perihelion has that three-star combination of being easier than it looks from below and superbly positioned. Found on the Tête D'Ane, less than 200 yards south of the car-park and quickly recognized from the coast path because of a rabbit's head – or a very bizarre donkey's head – formation above the cliff, it requires an abseil approach. Scramble down carefully past the rabbit's head and slightly to the left and you will see the top of an obvious corner. Abseil down this, or the wall to its left, to ledges just above the sea. Turning to face the cliff, a fine buttress to your left with a clean rectangular face and sharp arêtes to either side, becomes evident; Perihelion takes the right edge of the front face of this.

The route starts below a small but steep groove in the arête, and progress is quickly blocked by a bulge. However, there are excellent holds, and once on to the face proper, cracks in the arête lead more easily to the top. The protection is good, the position is excellent, and you can fully enjoy the sea foaming beneath you. If tempted, you can pause to survey the Ragged Edge, a committing and spectacular E5 that takes the left edge, or even Perry Coma (E5/6), a direct but sadly escapable line straight up the centre of the face. These two apart, the crag is covered in obvious crack-lines that all go at HVS. Perihelion must rank as one of the finest HVS climbs on British sea-cliffs.

Citizen's Edge is in many ways an unbalanced route: a technical crux, involving delicate laybacking up a rounded arête next to perfect protection, is followed by much easier but bolder climbing above. Facing north, it lacks some of the warmth and colour of Perihelion, however it shares the attributes of perfect rock and perfect position, and it is as clean a line as any draughtsman could wish for.

To reach Citizen's Edge, return to the car-park – where a handily placed ice cream van will tempt all but the keenest – and then follow the path north for about 70 yards, until an obvious detached triangle of rock can be seen below. Le Vyi is the cliff facing this triangle, with a narrow rocky summit easily gained from the coast path. Scramble down carefully to the left, facing out, until rocky steps lead to a large ledge system above a sheer drop. Citizen's Edge takes the slabby arête of the large buttress to your right. The base of the route is gained by traversing out from a smaller ledge beneath the thin slab that forms the western face of the cliff.

The lower half of the arête provides the technical crux. Increasingly poor layaways and rounded footholds lead up to a blank section at about 60 feet. Fortunately, small wires provide plentiful and sound protection. A combination of faith in the inherent friction of the granite and a palm wrapped lovingly around the arête brings curious flakelike mouldings to hand, and a possible belay. The original route then goes left under the overhang, before pulling over on excellent holds and following an easy crack and ledge system diagonally to the summit; better though to step up first and swing round on to the front face above the overhang. The climbing now is easier but quite bold, as you move up the edge of the buttress to another smaller overhang. Over this, slightly left of the arête, you can once again balance up the very edge of the face. Perfect friction makes the rounded holds feel more than adequate, and soon you are belayed to the summit flakes, your second out of sight and mind as you look out towards Guernsey and count the lobster pots.

Back to the car-park and more ice cream, and then a leisurely stroll south along the coast path, past the concrete lookout tower, left by the occupying German forces, and the gun barrels down at sea-level beneath the tower, dumped by rejoicing islanders, to the best cliff on the island, Le Pinacle. This is worth trying to spot from the boat or plane as you come into Jersey, for it is truly a stunning piece of rock: an immense standing wave of granite, barely attached to the island by a slim shoulder of grass, where Stone Age people manufactured axe heads and buried their dead. Two hundred feet high, the seaward face is seamed with bulges and tenuous flake-lines; there are very few apparent natural weaknesses. Indeed, there are few easy routes here, and they are unusually demanding for their grades! The rock is perfect, but it can be greasy before the sun has been on it. Beneath the crag, a sloping platform provides an excellent viewpoint, easily reached from the shoulder by walking round the northern end of the cliff.

The left-hand side of the face is slightly less steep, and a number of adventurous and excellent routes, such as Total Lack of Control (E2) lie here. But it is the superb central area that dominates your attention, and the continuously bulging line of flakes that forms Tax Exile is the stunning centre-piece – a route that ranks with the great Gogarth E5s for both quality of climbing and positions.

Just right of centre, at about 50 feet, a good ledge can be seen. This can be gained from directly below: a subtle leftwards rising groove-line, then a blank wall with a couple of long reaches at 6a, or by the obvious left-wards rising flakes at 4b. Above, the rock looks steep and forbidding, but the flakes offer the prospect of good holds and protection.

In fact, the holds are good; flaky jugs and positive footholds lead up to and through the first overhang to an uncomfortable resting position. Good protection is available, but it is well spaced, and a determined approach is essential. Now easier, but tiring, climbing up the rightwards-leaning flake leads to the second bulge. The holds are good, but as you pull up on undercuts, you can feel the effort of what has gone before. A bit of urgency should see you through to easier ground, and soon a ledge on the left provides both relief and a belay. Only now, looking down, do you realize how steep this pitch really is.

The top pitch, connecting a series of scoops to the right of the belay, is both on better rock and more enjoyable than it looks, and quickly leads to the summit – and it is a true summit – of Le Pinacle. An easy descent down the ridge to the Neolithic stones remains.

It seems remarkable that three such striking lines should have remained unclimbed until 1984, but that is all part of the attraction of Jersey. Where else could you climb on a crag the quality of Le Pinacle on an Easter Monday when the temperature touched 100°F (impressive enough in itself) *and* be completely alone! Not that climbers never visit the island: the history of climbing in Jersey records formative visits by Pat Littlejohn, Dominic Lee, Gary Gibson and Martin Crocker, as well as Al Rouse. All of these climbers are legendary for their determination and energy. My theory is that they were the only ones with the will-power to tear themselves from the beach!

Beachy Head

- ■ *LOCATION* • Beachy Head, directly west of Eastbourne, at the start of the South Downs. This is probably the biggest cliff on the south coast of England. The route described is opposite the lighthouse!
- ■ *ROUTES* • Monster Crack (XS 5c, 355 ft).

■ *FIRST ASCENTS* • M. Fowler, M. Morrison, C. Watts; December 1982.

■ *CONSIDERATIONS* • The chalk at Beachy Head is only loose on a totally massive scale. Coastguards should be forewarned (tel: 0323–20634), as an unwanted rescue would be embarrassing and probably quite dangerous. There is some risk of being hit by a stolen car while at the foot of the crag!

■ *GUIDEBOOK* • *Southern Sandstone* by Dave Turner (Climbers' Club, 1989).

IN DREAMS we create many complex images, and while dreaming we can see all of them clearly; but when we wake, maybe only one of those images lingers on in the daylight. Pilots of low-flying jets must have the same problem; like a captive audience watching a high-speed film, they see so much, each frame sharp; but afterwards, probably only milliseconds of memorable images survive, the rest fades into a blur.

I expect that if you were to fly low at high speed along the whole of the southern coastline of England, Dover to Land's End, there would only be one classic rock-climbing line that you would remember; one image that would truly be ingrained in your imagination – an enormous white wall, rising tall and long from a rocky beach, split cleanly by a single crack.

It took a true genius of the sport to see Monster Crack for what it is. The fact that the cliff is composed of chalk, that few climbers had been prepared to venture on to this medium, and that everybody assumed that it would be impossible to climb on these huge open faces because of a deep-rooted mistrust of their strength, was really irrelevant. The mythology surrounding figures like Aleister Crowley who had made previous forays at Beachy Head only obscures the fact that this is an enormous and steep cliff, crying out to be climbed. What Mick Fowler saw is a stunningly obvious crack splitting a wall that is huge and featureless; a classic natural line up a very steep cliff.

I first heard about Monster Crack from the Avon and Devon Adventure Seekers' Club, a crowd of harmless but talented lunatics who revel in the delights of loose rock, long runouts and spectacular and serious positions. While much of the country contemplates the encroaching threat of retro-bolting – making climbing 'safe' for the masses – of organized competitions, indoor gymnasia and a trend away from adventure, these individuals are happily pursuing a type of climbing more akin to alpinism. When told that one of the regular climbing magazines was about to publish a feature on adventure climbing, one of them replied, with a sigh, 'I suppose that will mean routes you have to put wires in.'

On-sight adventures, placing pegs en-route and cleaning away rubble with ice axes are all part of the fun to this breed. Monster Crack had been an easy and enjoyable day out.

I was intrigued; tales of a huge cliff, climbing on flints, ice screw belays – it sounded terrifying, but the enthusiasm in Dave's voice was infectious. A few photos later I was hooked – I had to go and climb Monster Crack.

In a way, making the commitment was the difficult part. Once I had made the decision, I knew I would get there eventually and do the route; details like 'when' and 'with whom' did not seem to matter. I eagerly took in all the advice Dave had to offer: 'You'll need a lump hammer to put the ice screws in, six pound should do … it's just that ice hammers don't give you enough clout, we only got them in an inch or so … and use some thick ropes, the flints are really sharp and it would be a bugger to cut through a rope up there … take a full set of Friends, and big wires, but nothing too small – anything less than about a Rock 4 will just rip out … and don't wear your best boots; there's nothing too technical – oh, and don't bother with a chalk bag!'

Not surprisingly, most of the people I tried to enthuse about the project were not too interested. Beachy Head is a long way away for anyone living north of Watford Gap, and this made excuses easy: 'It's a lot of effort for one route, isn't it?' I sympathized; it would be a weekend trip, and there wasn't much else down there to do, but I just knew it would be worth it. Deep down, perhaps I didn't really want to persuade anybody!

One evening, Andy mentioned he was going to London to see a crowd of his friends and celebrate his forthcoming marriage. Knowing that he would say 'yes' to any climbing project, I asked if the whole weekend was for drinking, or if he'd thought about getting a route in as well. Minutes later a plan was taking shape; I was to chaperone him on the Friday night, and we would climb Beachy Head on the Saturday. We'd be back home Saturday night. I set about gathering the gear, leaving Andy to phone the coastguard.

At Friday lunch-time, Andy phoned to say the coastguard was not amused: 'Well, I'll tell you what I told the others – you're quite mad. The whole cliff's falling apart; we've had three deaths already this year, one of them wasn't even wearing the right footwear for climbing!' As neither of us was aware of climbers being killed at Beachy Head, we thought the coastguard must have misinterpreted a few suicides. The atmosphere on the way down to London was a little nervous, nevertheless.

Saturday morning didn't dawn. Although the celebrations had remained for the most part civilized, it was lunch-time before either of us could drag our headaches out of bed, and we arrived at Beachy Head by a form of osmosis at about two o'clock. The journey had left us a little queasy, so a hearty meal in the clifftop pub was needed to inspire us to go and find the route. By the time we had got to the edge of the cliff, we were starting to liven up, and the sudden shock of seeing the main face was enough to set the adrenalin racing. I hadn't dreamed it was that big! Photographs often fail to give you a sense of proportion.

Now it was all excitement, as we rigged a quick abseil down an obvious gully. In fact, we chose a bad place, and the subsequent scramble down to the base of the cliffs was quite exhilarating in itself! By the time we were stood at the foot of the line, the nervousness of Friday afternoon had returned.

The guidebook gives the first pitch a technical grade of 5a. In fact, the technical grade is almost impossible to assess. The climbing is on small grassy tufts set in a steep slab, following an obvious rising line going up leftwards to the foot of the crack proper. If you are lucky, the ice-screw holes will be deep; for us they were barely an inch, and we tied the screws off to move quickly. Although the climbing is easy, it is a very frightening pitch – nothing feels as secure as you would like. But the belay ledge is a good size, and the ice-screw holes are now bigger, so that by the time you are both at the stance, your composure should have returned. Above, the crack soars upwards to an obvious roof.

And what a crack! You could almost forget that this was chalk, as you jam and wedge and thrutch, placing Friends and Hexcentrics. One hundred feet of fight and pleasure: the guidebook suggests two points of aid and 5b, but in fact it didn't seem out of place to use three. The exposure grows as the roof above gets bigger, until it blocks progress and forces you to belay. Again, there are sound holes to swallow your ice screws, but the comfortable feeling you had on the last stance is not there. There is a certain tension in your voice as you call down, 'Ready when you are, but don't fall off.' When you are both established beneath the roof, you wonder about the wisdom of thumping the rock and listening to the vibrations ripple across the face; how strong a rumble is needed to send the whole thing down ….

The next pitch feels serious, despite generally good protection and holds; it's just that the atmosphere is different – charged. You are aware of the importance of fate as you commit yourself to good, but hollow-sounding, blocks of chalk, as the crack-line skirts the roof to the left. The cave above, big enough to lie down and sleep in, feels like sanctuary, and you are soon happy again. It is only when your partner joins you that you realize there is no discernible way out.

The solution is outrageous. A footledge on the right wall of the cave can be traversed out to the arête, carefully caressing the flints that stick out from the chalk with your sticky fingers. Suddenly, there is 300 feet of space beneath you again, but this time there is no crack to try to cram your hands in, no slots to swallow your protection. Arms wrapped desperately round the arête, you look up and down, only to see a vertical wall of chalk, broken only occasionally by small flints. Keep calm, there is an ice screw, bedded to the eye, on the wall to the right. Reach up and finger the flints; which to use? The second snaps out of its socket at the slightest hint of a pull, and you wobble slightly on your airy perch. This is it; take a deep breath, focus your attention on that next ice-screw eye ten feet above … and go for it. The flints are small – all the larger ones must have gone on the first ascent – but they are enough. 5c climbing suitable for an indoor wall, little knobs of rock on a plain white background – how different can two similar situations be? With the ice-screw clipped, a measure of relief, and then a chalk jug – hooray – and the crack reappears. But wait a second, it is steeper now; throw a Moac in quickly and climb while you still can. Twenty feet to go, but the holds are only fair and the strain on the forearms is beginning to tell. A small ledge just below the top allows a moment of relief, and then you realize you've had your last protection; and the last few feet really are loose. Steady, as you pick your way up the inches between you and a long roll on the sweet, cropped grass above.

It seems hours later that you see your partner coming into focus. You untie the ropes and coil them slowly as the dark settles down. Little is said on the long drive home; there is little that needs saying. On the Sunday morning I woke with a smile, and though two people rang to entice me out to play, I stayed at home and read Kafka.

PEAK DISTRICT

The Burbage Valley

- **LOCATION** • The Burbage Valley, on the moors between Hathersage and Sheffield. Cars can be parked at either end, depending on which routes are planned.

- **ROUTES** • Long Tall Sally (E1 5b), The Rasp (E2 5b), Goliath (E5 6a), Silent Spring/Offspring (E4 5c/E5 6b).

- **FIRST ASCENTS** • Long Tall Sally – Alan Clarke (1960–65); The Rasp – Joe Brown, Don Whillans (1956); Goliath – Don Whillans (1958); Silent Spring – John Allen, Steve Bancroft (1975); Offspring – Johnny Dawes (1985).

- **CONSIDERATIONS** • The rock is perfect gritstone, quick drying in the summer months but exposed to wind.

- **GUIDEBOOK** • *Froggat*, ed. Keith Sharples (British Mountaineering Council, 1991).

THE GRITSTONE crags of Derbyshire flanking the moors south-west of Sheffield must be among the most developed and climbed-on cliffs in the world. I started to count the cars parked below Stanage edge one Sunday and gave up at 200, and there must be days when there are 1,000 people scrabbling away at this fine outcrop. Stanage has many good challenges, and attracts an amazing loyalty from its devotees. Every Christmas Day, come rain or shine, teams queue to ascend Christmas Crack. Climbers hitch out from Sheffield to spend hours on one boulder problem; others regularly achieve 100 routes in a day, with more ambitious climbers attempting the 'three-star routes in the 1983 guide' expedition. The four-mile-long edge has even been traversed!

Less popular with visitors, but dear to the hearts of more intense grit-stone aficionados is the Burbage Valley, a collection of outcrops and boulders with a couple of small quarries thrown in that together make up a wonderfully varied and beautiful gritstone playground. Easy of access, it is not uncommon to find the rocks deserted at six o'clock on a summer's evening, only to be teeming with boulderers 20 minutes later. For me, Burbage has always been evening rock, and for that reason it has also always been a one-route crag, where your goal is clear before you arrive. Mostly, I end up soloing and bouldering, just to warm up, and never get round to the route, so there are still plenty to do, but on a number of occasions I have had that 'best route I've ever done' feeling at Burbage, and in each case I am sure that the initial sense of purpose had something to do with it. Also, I can't help but feel that Burbage is a living example of the 'stone tape' theory, that somehow the rock has absorbed something of the character and atmosphere of the past and can replay it now, in the present.

Gritstone is about all sorts of things – simplicity of line for a start; short, obvious grooves that cry out for simple solutions, like Long Tall Sally. Standing beneath this perfectly shaped pitch, you can almost climb it in your head, the moves are so clear. However, gritstone also has a habit of throwing up unexpected problems, and on Long Tall Sally it is the bulge that somehow is harder than it should be. Easy moves lead you up to it, and good runners are easily arranged, but the predictable finger jams don't seem as good as you thought they'd be, and some real technique is needed for a few moves to bridge out and up into the beautiful groove above. Once established, the climbing reverts to the obvious, but the interest is maintained due to the tension in the calves and the need to press on before confidence fades. Although a mere 30 feet, the line is so elegant that it has to be a great climb, and so it is; but I only experienced the real power of the climb in my first ascent, trussed in a borrowed belt, spidery hemp rope hanging through the pitiful old Hexes I had almost certainly placed badly, as my bendy walking boots scratched away on the walls to either side. Every time I do this route now, I shiver and thank the stars for what must have been inspired luck that enabled me to walk away afterwards oblivious of the dangers I had put myself in. Watching Phil some four years later, wobbling like a terrified turkey on his first E1 lead, sighing with relief when he finally made it, memories of my first ascent returned.

Gritstone is about history, and about Joe Brown and Don Whillans in particular, and although you could pick any number of routes that bear their stamp, for me The Rasp at Higgar Tor says it all. The great leaning face that this route takes is now home to a number of fine hard climbs, but none of them has that quality that original solutions always have: while the Rasp tackles the face in the most obvious and direct manner, the other routes are all really just variations on a theme. Try to put yourself in the pioneers' position, with no chalk, Friends or fancy nuts, just simple boots and a single rope tied directly round your waist. Then look up at that awesomely steep face and contemplate falling 15 or more feet into space from the top of the flakes with that rope round your middle. Suddenly you understand why The Rasp was such an important ascent. It took me two attempts, with several years in between, and I ended up having to abseil for the gear both times. Only afterwards do you realize just how steep this crag is, with the swing once you have taken your first runner out worth every bit of the effort of the ascent. Anyone with a sense of history can't fail to get more out of this route than the great amount that they will have put in.

Strictly speaking, Joe is credited with The Rasp, but Don had his moments in the Burbage Valley too, and the finest can be found over at Burbage South, where the natural edge begins – a clean narrow chimney, narrowing slightly towards the top, and leaning slightly both to the right and over the vertical.

Gritstone is about commitment and no other route I have done involves more commitment than Goliath. Not just mental commitment, plenty of routes require your all in that department, but an all-round, body-and-soul fighting commitment; the sort that only something over-hanging, awkward and painful – not to mention frightening – can pro-voke. Very few people have grappled with this Whillans creation, and yet it is as obvious a line as you can imagine.

The first time I tried Goliath I had no idea what I was letting myself in for. Having hitched up to the Peak District one fine evening, I decided to stay the first night near the Fox House and ended up walking down the road late at night looking for somewhere to stay. I followed a track up and right and ended up at the Burbage quarries. In the morning, with more enthusiasm than sense, I put on a pair of boots and headed for Above and Beyond the Kinaesthetic Barrier, a classic boulder problem I had heard much about. Being completely unable to work this out, I gave up and began looking around for something else. Without any serious intentions, I started up Goliath. It seemed easy enough – a bit graunchy, but my shoulder and leg style seemed fairly secure – and I was soon fair-ly comfortable at half height, where a good foothold makes the position almost restful ... for a few minutes, at least.

At this point, I wanted to get back down quickly. The chimney above is narrower, and the way it leans makes any progress precarious. The trouble is, it is quite frightening going down from there, the best method being a good clean jump. Eventually, I plucked up courage and leapt, walking away without any ill effects.

When I came back ten years later, I was armed with a Camalot 4 and plenty of determination, having recently had an off-width, crack-bashing session at Curbar and in North Wales. My first attempt was no better for the intervening years and fancy gear. As soon as I got to the footledge, I realized that the Camalot was pitifully inadequate for the next few feet, and it would only come into play nearer the top, although I had been warned that the top was actually the crux, so it wasn't all bad. Ten years had done nothing to my joints though, and an unnecessary fall from

Brown's Eliminate at Froggatt had left my back less resistant to such a tumble, and it took me a few minutes to pick myself up from the ground, intact but in some pain; whatever else happened, I wasn't going to be able to jump off again!

Twenty minutes or so later, after spotting Phil on an unsuccessful attempt at Above and Beyond (which I still can't do, and have given up trying), I was ready for another go. This time I committed myself to the crack above the rest, and the next 15 minutes seemed to last for ever. All I will say is that when the Camalot eventually goes in, you are really glad of it; and as for the climbing, I can't begin to describe the pain my shoulder was in for the next four days. Dress up as well, this is one for those thick fibre-pile trousers you used to love wearing, and any additional bandaging you put round your knees will help.

Gritstone is also about being gripped, and about subtle moves requiring fine balance and faith. For any keen gritstone climber in the late 1970s, the routes that were inspiring us all were the creations of John Allen and Steve Bancroft. Again, there are many routes that you could use to illustrate their contribution to the art of gritstone climbing, but Silent Spring is one of the very finest and is quite unusual in concept as well. Burbage South has two quarries at its right-hand end, the southernmost of which is dominated by a huge block, apparently suspended in mid-air. In fact, the block is home to a number of routes unique to Peak District gritstone in that they require an abseil approach. Silent Spring is an elegant solution to the problem of how to climb on the block without this approach; it traverses on from one side, and in two bold pitches it takes in the longest face of the block, before finishing up the obvious arête.

The important thing to consider when attempting Silent Spring is that nobody else should be about. The likelihood of calling for a top rope is thereby reduced to zero and you can get used to the fear and concentrate on the climbing. It isn't that hard, but it is delicate and there isn't any point at which you are happy about making a mistake. I was silly enough to be offered the second pitch and accepted; not silly because the second pitch is the harder to lead, but because the first is by far the harder to second! By the time I got to the security of the hanging-rope belay, I was almost ready to quit, but the smile on Tom's face was so huge that I couldn't quit without at least trying.

Slowly I stepped rightwards, arriving without further incident at the infamous 'reverse mantelshelf'. With the security of the old bolts above, this seemed a simple move, and the rest of the pitch flowed easily. Tom couldn't contain his excitement on the top, and we ran almost the whole way to the Fox House in giddy spirits.

At the time, I assumed that I would do nothing else on the block, but then I heard about Offspring, a Johnny Dawes creation that traverses on where Silent Spring goes up, and takes in some sensational positions on the side-wall of the block. Initially graded E6 6c, I had no real ambitions in that direction, but I was still intrigued. A few years later, I did the bril-

liant Wall Street Crash at Millstone (also originally graded E6 6c), and
started to think it may be possible to do Offspring after all. I knew a few
people had repeated it, and the reports were not all bad. The deal was
clinched when Paul came to stay one day with Offspring on his mind.
We headed out for Burbage.

Gritstone is about making decisions and then following them through
100 per cent. A quick look over the top brought back the doubts I had
previously had, it looked very steep down there. After abseiling down to
a secure belay on the arête and getting comfortable, Paul set off down the
curving crack. The jams are fair, but the wall is very steep, and there are
only scratchings for the feet. So you arrive at the best jams, at the point
where you start going up, quite pumped. Paul duly fired a Friend in the
break and then almost casually grabbed the karabiner. 'I'm too pumped,'
he said. 'I'll just clip in and take a rest.'

The next three minutes were hilarious. Try as he might, he couldn't
take a hand off long enough to pull a rope up into the karabiner, and
when he did, he couldn't open the gate because he was hanging from it
with the other arm. His face went through the whole range from
pumped to gripped to resigned, and eventually, with a suitably loud
scream, he let go. The swing is impressive, as anyone who has seen the
Stone Monkey video will know.

I lowered Paul to the ground, declined a go on the sharp end myself
and top roped it, just to get the Friend, of course. Unbelievably, it really
wasn't that bad; you had to keep going when it mattered, but it was all
there. I secretly resolved to return without Paul and amaze somebody
else with a 'flashed' ascent.

That's how it should have been too, but in fact it took three attempts
next time round, the difference between top roping and leading. On the
first two, I just couldn't get that image of Paul flying downwards out of
my head, and Offspring punishes hesitations. For anybody shorter than
six feet, the E6 6c grade must surely still be true as well, so don't be too
fooled by the relaxation in grade.

Burbage is still a regular venue for me, although I seem to climb less
and walk more each year. On a snowy winter's day I can scramble along
the foot of the crags with my dogs and hear the gritstone calling out to
me with echoes of the past. Each time, I look up at the next challenge and
think of the future.

Chee Dale

- **LOCATION** • Chee Dale, where the River Wye runs between Topley Pike on the A6, three miles east of Buxton, and Miller's Dale on the B6049.

- **ROUTES** • Sirplum (E1 5b), Mad Dogs and Englishmen (E3 5c), Clarion Call (E5 6a), The Golden Mile (E5 6b).

- **FIRST ASCENTS** • Sirplum – Bob Dearman, R. Brown (1964); Mad Dogs and Englishmen – Gabe Regan, Al Evans (1976); Clarion Call – Gary Gibson (1983), Nick Dixon (1984); The Golden Mile – Pete Livesey, A. Livesey (1980).

- **CONSIDERATIONS** • The rock in Chee Dale varies from superb to terrible, with Sirplum having a bit of both. Approach from the Buxton end of the dale, parking at the top or the bottom of Topley Pike, and using the old railway line.

- **GUIDEBOOKS** • *Chee Dale* (British Mountaineering Council, 1987); *Peak Limestone* by Alan James (Vertical Brain, 1992).

THE PEAK DISTRICT is littered with limestone cliffs, and many of them are excellent. High Tor is a magnificent face, with almost every route oozing quality. Stoney Middleton has all the history you could want, and still attracts huge numbers on to its polished classics. The ugly Raven Tor epitomizes the easy access 'rock gymnast' mentality, with some particularly hard routes struggling up the first few feet of the central section. All of these are popular, and in their own way deservedly so. Yet each has only a limited number of routes, and none can provide the seemingly inexhaustible amount of rock found in the valley of Chee Dale.

The best approach is from the western end of the dale, at Topley Pike. The A6 from Buxton follows the Wye for about three miles, and then cuts rightwards up a steep hill, Topley Pike. There is a car park at the foot and at the top of the hill, and the longer flat walk from the former should be judged against the quick slide but steep hike back to the latter; either way, the aim is to gain the old railway, formerly part of the London to Manchester line, from which all the buttresses can be reached easily. Except in the best conditions, a pair of wellingtons can prove useful, as crossing the river is necessary to climb on some areas. The footpath that follows the river itself is gradually being upgraded by conservation volunteers, but many parts of the path are very muddy for most of the year, particularly opposite Chee Tor.

Once on the railway, all the crags are quickly reached. The first into view, and one of the most dramatic buttresses in the Peak District, is Plum Buttress, a giant prow of rock perched atop a 60-foot wall. The fact that the base of the cliff is a steep slope itself seems to lend the buttress even more height, and not surprisingly the routes here have an almost 'mountaineering' feel. More surprising are some reasonably graded routes that explore positions on the central nose, and both Sirplum and Aplomb are outstanding. Despite Sirplum being a well-documented line, it is strange that neither sees much traffic, because for position and audacity they must be two of the finest E1s in the country.

Sirplum is the best of the two, being slightly more committing and impossible looking! The route starts on a good ledge to the right of the huge nose, at the height of the very obvious break that runs under the roofs. A short but difficult wall, the technical crux, leads up to the next break, and it is vital to place good protection here to encourage your second. I have rescued two nervous seconds who have been faced with huge pendulums if they failed on this crux, and both had had to give more than moral support to their leaders, so be thoughtful! Now relax and trend leftwards and upwards, past an incredibly positioned ledge to a huge thread runner in the next break, at a small roof. Look left: yes, it does go out there! The holds are enormous, but the exposure makes you pull so hard that you tire quickly, so relax again, try not to think about how difficult it would be to regain the rock if you fall off and move left to the edge of everything. Putting aside doubts about the rock (which are quite valid, despite the fact that nobody ever seems to pull off holds), climb the groove above to the top, and a quiet corner where you can recover your composure and reflect upon a route from 1964. Would you have been happy without all that modern gear?

If you are one of those people who genuinely revel in this sort of thing, then an abseil descent is a must, followed by Aplomb, preferably in training shoes and without Friends! This unsung gem traverses the break between the roofs from left to right, finishing up Sirplum, although it is possible to go direct from the huge thread on Sirplum to the top at the same grade. Whatever your thoughts, make sure you take in the line of Sloe Gin that breaches the huge roofs directly beneath the top groove of Sirplum, and provides one of the best 'modern' bolt-protected lines in the dale.

Continuing down the railway line, the next buttresses – the sunny Sidings on the left, and the elevated Moving Buttress on the right – provide a number of enjoyable climbs, though they contain no real classics. On reaching the first tunnel, the railway can be quitted for a path to the right, that drops beneath the Embankment, a curious cliff, neglected for years but now a sport-climbing complex, with many modern additions and a curiously intense character. Opposite, you can see the Long Wall, a more aesthetic and solid version of the Embankment. The next crag along though is the magnificent Two Tier Buttress, with its obvious wooded terrace dividing the two tiers towards the left-hand end.

Two Tier Buttress is the Curbar edge of limestone, the crag where everything is hard (whatever its grade) and where any indecision is punished. The rock is superb, and the climbing is always committing. There are a number of important classics here, but the finest has to be Mad Dogs and Englishmen, a superb and intricate route that winds its way up the right-hand end of the buttress. After a bold start to gain the first flake-line, it is always well protected and has a number of good rests. However, the climbing is tricky, and there is plenty of it. The initial traverse left to the second flake is the crux for most people, and can be climbed high or low. The polish on the footholds makes the moves feel hard for 5c, but there is a wire runner directly above you. The moves over the central roof are actually the easiest on the climb, due to a superb hidden jug; from the ledge above, a traverse back right is easier, but beware the top groove! It is not uncommon for leaders to fail on the last few moves, where some large holds should compensate for a slight steepening of angle.

The river can be crossed on wobbly stepping stones just beneath the lowest point of Two Tier Buttress, which lead to Max Buttress. This gives excellent bouldering as well as a number of bold pitches on superb compact rock. Walking down the path, more stepping stones lead to the Nook, a fierce little crag with some powerful roof climbing, with the unusual Nettle Buttress on the other side of the river. A bridge crosses the river, and at the next bridge the path splits. Stay on the right-hand side for Chee Tor, cross the bridge and follow more stepping stones for the Cornice.

The Cornice is a bizarre crag. Completely wet for up to six months of the year, with the most amazing fringe of icicles in cold winters, it has a brief but very active summer life. For a few short months it is cleaned, smudged with chalk, draped with ropes and venerated by hordes of climbers. Then, despite being untouched by the heaviest summer storm, it succumbs again to autumnal seepage, and hibernates through another winter and spring. Partly because of its character, and partly because it is an incredibly steep and impressive crag, its history is interesting. Despite some aid exploits in the early 1960s, and a smattering of basically free climbs in the late 1970s, the real potential of the crag was not apparent until Gary Gibson made his Clarion Call with five bolt runners in 1983. What stunned other climbers was that such a steep and normally wet cliff could yield a classic route at the relatively mild grade of E4 6a: within weeks it had become very popular, receiving up to five ascents in one day.

Not everybody was happy though: the problem was the bolt runners. At this time, bolts had been used on only a few routes, and then only sparingly, as a last resort. Gibson had taken a new approach, ignoring the potential for natural or even peg protection, arguing that the result justified the means. It was a short-lived sensation: Paul Mitchell removed the bolts, threatening to remove any future ones, and the winter seepage set in. Gibson had seen the potential though, and all he needed at the start of the next year was for climbers to rally to his call for a massive campaign of bolt-protected routes to begin.

Surprisingly, with hindsight, Peak District climbers were not ready for bolting to become an acceptable practice, and the next season began with Nick Dixon making a very bold lead of Clarion Call with three peg runners, the first of which was very poor. At E6 there were few takers, and Gibson's second ascent of the route in its new form seemed to signal agreement that the bolting initiative had lost. Not for long though: in 1985 Gibson sportingly bolted Cosmopolitan, E6 and brilliant, heralding a new surge in popularity for bolt-protected routes and this time really opening people's eyes to what was possible. It worked, and four years later two bolts were replaced in Clarion Call, with two pegs protecting the upper section. As 1992 came to an end, a third bolt was replaced, and by 1994 bolts had replaced the two pegs: the wheel has come full circle.

Despite all the history, or perhaps because of it, Clarion Call is an excellent route. By no means as hard, or as impressive, as some of the modern additions, it still makes a committing challenge. Who can say at which stage it was best? You will have to ask yourself that after climbing it, but I can't help feeling that there probably is an optimum number of bolts in such a climb, and it currently has too many. Cosmopolitan is a good example of how sparse bolting can create a brilliant and thrilling route, and it is revealing that the well-bolted, yet slightly harder, direct finish to Cosmopolitan receives many, many more ascents than the original route!

Directly opposite the Cornice is the fine Chee Tor, hosting the highest concentration of classics in the dale. There are too many good routes here to comment on them all, but in both the E3 and E5 grades the choice is superb. In complete contrast to the Cornice, the rock here is mainly vertical, and the natural protection opportunities are better. Consequently, many of the best routes pre-date the advent of bolt protection, and despite arguments over two routes in recent years, Chee Tor has become established as a minimal-bolt-only crag. The big threat for a place like this is retro-bolting, and as a number of the E5s have scary sections, they are obvious candidates for such a totally retrograde step. Hopefully, the popularity of these routes in their present state will deter anybody from such a pointless act. One of the routes that many visitors to the tor show interest in is The Golden Mile. Being positioned on an impeccable wall of milky-white rock, it cries out to be climbed, and provides a difficult and exciting pitch. However, it is beautifully balanced, with a technical, but safe, crux followed by a thrilling top section.

The route begins up an obvious shallow groove, just right of the bulging arête of Mortlock's Arête, the E4 that thinks it's an E5! The groove is much trickier than it looks, but at its top a step right leads to a rest and good runners. Above, a thread runner usually hangs from a small ledge. Most climbers work up to the right of this and reach left to clip the thread before stepping back down for a rest, but it is just as easy to step slightly left and go straight up, aiming to get your fingers in the pocket the thread is hung from before clipping. A friend of mine did this when the thread was missing, and then had the problem of threading a wire through the pocket with two of his fingers jammed in it! Either way, the next moves are the crux. The aim is to get stood on the small ledge, and the holds above do not seem to help: a reach up right followed by a rockover leftwards should do the trick though, and a small flake seems to accept a Rock One once you are stood up. Teeter leftwards to a better hold and compose yourself.

Most people spend a long time here fiddling with runners. I don't suppose it would change things if they were told that these runners always fall out when, having pulled up a few moves, you step back right and face the second crux. A panic here will result in a spectacular plummet, but there are good holds if you can sort out your hands in time to find them! A few seconds later, you will have reached a decision about retro-bolting, one way or another, depending upon whether you are at the belay in the break or uncomfortably close to the ground!

It is hard to forecast the future of Chee Dale. Sport-climbing is well established, and the wealth of unclimbed rock in the dale will encourage further bolting. It is difficult enough to picture climbing Sirplum in 1964, in plimsolls, with hemp rope; modern equipment has altered that experience for ever. The Golden Mile is much as it was on the first ascent, though; it would be a shame if that experience were to be lost too.

Wimberry

■ **LOCATION** • Wimberry rocks, high on the Chew Valley skyline above Greenfield. Park at the Dovestones reservoir, just off the A635.

■ **ROUTES** • Freddie's Finale (HVS 5b), Blasphemy (E2 5c), Wristcutter's Lullaby (E6 6c).

■ **FIRST ASCENTS** • Freddie's Finale – Joe Brown (1948); Blasphemy – John Allen, Steve Bancroft, Neil Stokes (1973); Wristcutter's Lullaby – Nick Plishko (1987).

■ **CONSIDERATIONS** • The rock is rough hard gritstone, quick drying in the summer but often bitterly cold in winter, as it faces north-east and it is high up.

■ **GUIDEBOOK** • *Moorland Gritstone: Chew Valley* by Chris Hardy and Carl Dawson (British Mountaineering Council, 1989).

A VERY small number of people believe that Wimberry is one of the most impressive crags in the Peak District; some of them even say that it contains the Peak's finest gritstone routes – very odd for a crag that is positively arctic in climate all winter, faces north-east and thus misses the best of the summer sun, and that requires an exhaustingly steep slog to approach it. The fact that the routes might be good would not be enough to draw out such accolades, for places like the ever-popular Millstone and much visited Roaches all have superb routes. So what is it about Wimberry that is so special?

The Wimberry experience is very different from the one you can gain at most Peak gritstone edges. I was first introduced to it by a friend who had recently moved to Mossley, overlooking the Chew skyline. Mark was naturally enthusiastic about everything – as only a triathlete can be – but I needed some convincing.

'You've just got to come over to Wimberry, it's just the best crag in the world,' he said on the phone one Tuesday evening.

By this I understood that it was the most recent crag he had visited.

'OK,' I replied reluctantly, not for the first time; a night out with Mark is always fun, even though my expectations, based on past experiences, didn't match his enthusiasm. 'Half-past six tomorrow, I'll come to your place.'

'That's great, we can cycle over to Greenfield and then … '

'Mark, I have a car: we'll drive!'

'Sure, OK, well, the crag is just near the road so we should get a full evening.'

It was September – dark by eight-thirty. I arrived as promised at six-thirty. We drove over to the Dovestones reservoir, and I couldn't believe I had fallen for it again.

'Mark, it's miles away!' I joked, looking up to what seemed a very distant horizon.

'No, we start bouldering here and work our way up: be there in no time,' he replied, as if he really believed it.

What followed was the best bouldering session I had ever had, as Mark led me round a Fontainebleau-style circuit, slowly gaining height as we climbed, until, as darkness enveloped us completely, we were still a long way off from Wimberry itself, but it really didn't matter. Mark had little difficulty in persuading me back the following Sunday, when we aimed to reach the crag first and boulder on the way down.

Although the evening sun had warmed the boulders that Wednesday, the sky threatened rain on the Sunday morning and I packed a waterproof jacket as a precaution. By ten o'clock I was walking up to Wimberry with Mark, and I was cold. By twelve o'clock we had failed on two routes and it was snowing. Other friends who went to Millstone laughed the next day when I tried to describe how cold it had been. Perhaps it had been a freak storm, so I pledged myself for the following Sunday when Mark rang again on Tuesday night.

That Sunday everything went to plan, and, on a perfect gritstone day with no one else around, I finally climbed on Wimberry: The Trident, Blue Lights Crack and the immaculate Route One all gave in fairly gracefully, though Blue Lights kept a portion of flesh as a memento. We moved round to Freddie's Finale, a Joe Brown route from 1948 and an awkward-looking line. Mark had failed on this before, so he sorted his gear out knowingly and carefully wrapped a plaster round a small wound on his hand from Blue Lights .

By this time another team had arrived, and the air was full of encouragement as Mark began to climb. Swiftly, he established himself below the bulge, and arranged a runner. The grunting started, and continued for a very long time. Finally, with no further runners and his plaster missing, he heaved his upper body round the bulge and threw a leg out leftwards on to the slab. Impressed by his determination, I decided to second rather than lead.

Reluctant to sink my fists deep into the crack where the rock can nibble away at the soft skin, I opted for a strange mixture of chimneying and wedging that had done the job before in similar positions. However, the crack leans too sharply to the left, and I soon ended up stuck: not just puzzled, not just unsure about what to do next, but well and truly stuck. My shoulder and elbow were squeezed into the crack, one leg securely wedged and the other useless beneath, and I realized that the only movement I could make was downwards. Mark started to laugh, and I joined in out of a sense of camaraderie. There was nothing else to do, so with a quick 'I'm off,' I dislocated myself from the rock and fell across and down almost to the ground.

I could tell from his silence that Mark was pleased, so I went back up there quickly, and annoyed. That time it was jams all the way and the bulge passed smoothly, with only a trickle of blood. We were both cut and bruised, so when Mark proposed a descent and some bouldering, I was more than happy. A route where aggression pays, perhaps, but Freddie's Finale is no soft HVS – one of those classical HVS routes like Octo on Cloggy: 'the HVS that thinks it's an E1'. Sound fist-jamming technique is not the sort of thing you need often nowadays.

The Chew Valley is quiet; not in terms of the hordes who gather down at the reservoir or the squads of children who wander up the brook looking for bathing pools in summer, but in terms of the number of climbers you will find on any crag at a particular time. Wimberry may be the finest crag, but the popularity afforded it is derisory compared to the eastern edges. It is possible to wander for hours along the upper Chew edges and see no climbers at all. Very occasionally, you will meet a couple of teams who have all had the same idea as you, but the peace will still largely remain unbroken, for they will have come here for that too. Wandering around the Chew Reservoir as it got dark that evening, I knew I had found a spot to treasure.

My next visit was several summers later. Mark had moved off to new challenges on the other side of the world, and I kept trying to save the Chew for special days, only to be unable to persuade anybody to go with me. Eventually a new guidebook did the trick, and I found myself beneath Blasphemy, a route I remembered Mark had pointed to as being another long-standing feud of his. Fortunately, I picked the right techniques first time, and the climbing went smoothly. It is hard to describe how good this route is, superbly varied as it is; suffice it to say that there are few better E2 5c routes on gritstone.

After frightening ourselves silly on Sick Bay Shuffle and the desperate Consolation Prize, we were running out of steam. A top rope on the impressive 'Desecration' wall seemed an obvious way of extending the climbing with minimal nervous energy, so I walked round and managed to set up an extremely complicated multi-point belay with two top ropes, one towards the left-hand side above the roof, and the other towards the right-hand side, clipped below the roof. The plan was to have a look at any of the ground on the Neptune's Tool, Berlin Wall and Wristcutter's Lullaby routes. Although clearly improbable, we both felt that there had to be holds up there somewhere, and we were keen to see what sort of shape and size they took.

What we found was some of the trickiest and best gritstone climbing either of us had ever done – wonderful pockets and pebbles, and surprisingly good gear placements. We soon realized that Wristcutter's Lullaby was the line of the buttress, although neither of us dared try the hideous-looking roofs that cap the route. After a couple of attempts, I had worked out most of the moves on the wall below the break, and I felt that I wanted to leave it there and come back one day to lead it from the ground. I am sure that if I ever do I will be pleased enough to forget my previous inspection: I am also sure that the upper section will provide more than enough excitement on sight.

Wristcutter's Lullaby and the hanging arête of Appointment with Fear must be among the most sensational high-grade gritstone routes around. Yet Wimberry is a superb place whatever your standard. From Route One upwards, the place has an almost mountainous charm, with superb views, peace and no little effort needed to get there. With the added attraction of superb bouldering on the slopes below, and numerous smaller crags dotted around the Chew skyline in the unlikely event of a surge in popularity, why doesn't it get the recognition it deserves?

YORKSHIRE

FOR MANY years the Right Wing at Malham Cove represented the very epitome of limestone climbing. Many of the routes there became coveted test-pieces, and in the late 1970s ascents of Slender Loris or Limehill were of some significance. The rock was of such a high quality and so compact that good sections had no cracks at all. Consequently, many of the routes sported bold moments, and the angle was sustained enough to get most leaders pumped, resulting in some spectacular falls. By the early 1980s these routes were becoming popular, and there were always good numbers of climbers based on the large picnic rock beneath the face, and at least two ropes getting all tangled up round the roof of Carnage.

Times change: the Right Wing now is usually remarkably quiet, and there is certainly always room on the picnic stone. Attention for the last few years – and almost certainly for the next few as well – is firmly fixed on the Central Walls, with their plethora of modern sports climbs. The 1992 *Yorkshire Limestone* guide jokes that two of these routes, Consenting Adults and Bolt Revolt, 'must account for half of the climbing done in Yorkshire'. Certainly, the apparently incessant stream of suitors for these routes is quite entertaining when similarly graded and infinitely finer, longer routes are just over 50 yards away. The lure of the quick clip, the opportunity to lower back to the ground, to share in the camaraderie of the catwalk, to show off your latest designer muscles or even tights must be very powerful. I shouldn't mock, for I have been just as guilty, and thoroughly enjoy visiting the catwalk at the end of the day, when it is a little less crowded, for a quick route or two. It is more than a problem of fashion though: the fundamental restructuring of limestone climbing in England that took place at Malham in the mid-1980s, following on from Pen Trwyn a few years earlier, has long-term consequences that we can only guess at.

For me, the problem with the sport routes at Malham is not the climbing, the rock or the ethics: it is the mentality of some of the people who sheepishly see no other rock here. The general atmosphere on the catwalk can be quite claustrophobic at times, particularly if a number of parties are fishing for the same route. The sight of a group of six climbers arguing over who was to have next 'go' at a route 30 feet long (when none of them had got further than 15 feet up the route on previous attempts) is one that has left me saddened in the extreme. Certainly, this is not true of all climbers who visit here, or of those who seem to live there, and it has to be said that I have also seen some inspirational sights on the routes here, including some staggeringly determined on-sight attempts that really showed the sort of willpower that some modern routes demand. Perhaps there will come a time when standards generally are high enough for the Lower Central Wall to be looked at in terms of the quality of its climbing, rather than because of its *in situ* gear; until then I can't help but feel it will continue to be over-popular and over-crowded, while the Right Wing will remain peaceful.

Of the many routes on the Right Wing that deserve attention, my favourites are Wombat and Midnight Cowboy. Both are classic outings at the top end of their respective grades, and even though both are essentially safe, they have exciting moments.

Wombat's moments start on the ground, with a bold and quite committing sequence up a polished and awkward wall into the bottom of a groove. A tree used to sprout from the foot of this groove, and lassoing it was almost as much fun as climbing up to it with the top rope protection it provided, but now it is necessary to climb without error or fuss into the sanctuary of bridging that the groove contains. You will know after

one attempt whether you will be able to do the route today, because failure here is likely to be painful, if not dangerous. Once in the groove, a
pleasantly strenuous and well-protected E1 climb unfolds, with good
laybacks and bridging soon leading to a small bulge, a step right and
soon a good resting ledge. Above, the climb gets trickier. Make sure you
place good protection here, as the next few moves feel committing, and
the top wall has a habit of spitting off nervous climbers. The short corner
above is climbed, and on out leftwards until a rounded break is reached:
some fiddly runners here protect the crux above. If necessary, it is possible to reverse back down a few feet and rest a while, after feeling out the
holds above the break. The problem seems to be that, after a good jug,
there are nothing but small finger pockets, and the top of a route like this
is not where you want to be hanging around on small finger pockets.
What you don't know, however, is that there are also some big holds on
that upper wall, cunningly disguised. Have confidence, guess correctly
and you will soon be palming the top, admiring the way the rabbits keep
the croquet lawn up there so smooth.

Midnight Cowboy is a different beast, adding a considerable degree of
exposure into the equation. More of an expedition this, especially if you
have not been up on the Terrace Wall before: just watching the kids sitting on the edge of the cove frightens me, and I found a rope a big comfort just to get to the foot of the climbs. From the right-hand end of the
terrace, an obvious ledge system continues out above the void past a
tree. Using any method you like, get out to a flake about 20 feet right of
the tree and take a belay. Going up looks uninviting from here, so make
sure the right person has got the job of leading! The rock here, at the end
of the terrace wall, is as perfect as you can get, and the combination of
thuggy pulls to leave the belay, followed by a bold and very technical
but delicate ramp, feet on scoops and fingers on tiny edges, culminating
in an explosive layback up an overhanging flake, makes an instant classic. Why is Bolt Revolt more popular than this?

Although Malham was the initial focus of the bolting craze that
seemed to sweep Yorkshire in the mid-1980s, no single route seems to
sum up the ethical dilemmas that have arisen as a result of bolts than
Frankie … at Kilnsey. Originally climbed as a hard and serious aid route
in November 1984 by Duncan Drake and Alan Stevenson, Frankie Comes
to Kilnsey, as it was named, was a route firmly in the style of a tradition
of Yorkshire climbing that dated back to the 1950s and 1960s. Although
the popular trend in 1984 was to free old aid routes – this was the year
Martin Berzins almost freed Dominatrix at the same crag – the two
climbers involved had pioneered a number of very bold and serious aid
climbs over the preceding two years, characterized by marginal peg
placements and hook moves. As no bolts were used on Frankie Comes to
Kilnsey, the two aid climbers might justifiably feel proud of a boldly con-
ceived climb that seems to extend and develop the aid-climbing ethic
that was long established in Yorkshire. I certainly remember aiding
Controversy at Malham (later to become the famous Cry Freedom as a

free route) in 1984 and, despite employing some drilled threads, that too was a very bold route: aid climbing was still an acceptable practice, and seemed to have a future, albeit a limited one.

However, 1984 was also the year that the first free-climbing bolt was placed at Kilnsey, when Pete Gomersall put a single bolt in his Zero Option. It was perhaps inevitable, given that Frankie took a line up a basically vertical wall directly to the Balas bolts, and was therefore very accessible to top-rope attempts, that somebody would look at Frankie as a free-climbing possibility. As it was, Gomersall was not only keen to free-climb the route, he took the bull by the horns and placed three bolts, effectively creating the crag's first modern sport climb. As with Clarion Call in Chee Dale, opinion was divided as to the validity of this action, and after a brief period of popularity the aid climbers involved removed the bolts, furious that their efforts in creating a hard and serious aid climb had been ruined. It was left to Martin Berzins, as guardian of ethics, to step in only two months after Gomersall's ascent and climb the route free. Critics were quick to note that Berzins' ascent was not in very good style, and without more thought the bolts went back in.

This saga might have ended there but for Martin's devilish determination, and so the bolts were to come out again, preceding a clean ascent. Frankie Comes Too Soon, as the route was briefly known, was graded E6, and required unusual runner placements and some prior knowledge. The argument that the route was actually better as an E5 that could be attempted truly on sight was a powerful one, though, and before long the bolts went back in. The *Yorkshire Limestone Supplement* of 1987 summed it up thus: 'it may be argued that the route should never have been pegged; that once pegged it should never have been bolted; once bolted should not have been de-bolted and should have been initially climbed with more daylight'. The story doesn't end there, and in fact has still not ended: the bolts have been in and out of the route a number of times since then.

The sad thing about all this is that Frankie ... is an excellent piece of climbing. The moves are continually interesting, and the angle is not so steep that you wither instantly; rather it provides a cumulative wearing down of energy that means that even if you pass the crux (easier for the tall), you may well fail on the easier upper wall. To make matters worse, there is a blind move near the top that is hard on a first attempt, and even if you do reach the bolt on Balas, you've still got the desperate crux on that route to do. I did the route with bolts and enjoyed it. I would not have tried it without bolts in place, although I may well have top roped it in that state, having just done Balas. I can't tell you if the bolters or de-bolters, or even the aid climbers, were right or wrong. I can tell you that the continual hammering the rock is getting is leaving an ugly mess, and so it might be an idea to agree once and for all what is to happen to the route. My feelings are that it should stand as a bold unbolted route, a tribute to Berzins' efforts, and if people want to do the climb, it is easy enough to set up a top rope.

The other of the 'Big Three' Yorkshire limestone crags is Gordale Scar, and it is perhaps fitting that one of the best routes in Yorkshire should be found here – free-climbing an old aid route using the *in situ* rubbish of a generation ago as partial protection, but relying on natural protection to back it up. For all the arguments about bolt protection and making routes accessible to on-sight attempts, Cave Route (Right Hand) stands out as a masterpiece of the new style of climbing squashed into the old ethics. Gymnastic and strenuous climbing (and so much of it that), like a good hill, you feel you have finished the pitch at least twice before the cave finally arrives, placed in majestic surroundings and taking what by any standards is a fantastic natural line: this route has it all. And if you want to aid up it in the winter, you can do that too, on natural placements and using the same rotting tat and ironmongery as the free climber.

The stories about the first ascent – Livesey jumping for an aid climber's rope and his protégé, Fawcett, eventually freeing the route on his honeymoon – somehow just add to the route: here is something special that top climbers were chasing for years. Try this one on sight and you can feel their sweat and share an experience very similar to theirs, for little in the way of protection and fashion has altered Cave Route. The same isn't true about the rest of Yorkshire.

NORTHUMBERLAND

■ **LOCATION** • Sandy Crag, high up on the moor east of the B6341, north of Elsdon; about 35 miles north-west of Newcastle-upon-Tyne.

■ **ROUTES** • Angel Fingers (E1 5b, 65 ft); Sandy Crack (E2 5b, 70 ft); Greenford Road (E5 6b, 75 ft).

■ **FIRST ASCENTS** • Angel Fingers , Sandy Crack – John Earl, Bob Hutchinson (1975/6); Greenford Road – Bob and Tommy Smith (1980).

■ **CONSIDERATIONS** • The rock is fairly clean, hard sandstone, quick drying and getting any available afternoon sun. A breeze is helpful in keeping insects away in the summer months. Access involves trampling across a large heather moor; gamekeepers enforce the 1 March to 31 July ban due to grouse breeding.

■ **GUIDEBOOK** • Northumberland Climbing Guide, ed. John Earl (Northumberland Mountaineering Club, 1989).

ONE OF the great charms of climbing in Northumberland is the tremendous sense of isolation felt at places like Sandy Crag. While the more
well-known crags of Bowden Doors and Kyloe are still very quiet compared to many areas of the country, you will usually find somebody
there if you visit on a fine day. At Sandy Crag though, a visit on your
own could result in an epic fight for survival if you slipped and broke an
ankle. Not that it is particularly remote, but the lack of paths, the hidden
holes and boulders in the knee-high heather and the small number of
routes lead even the most dedicated of locals here only very occasionally.

This may seem unduly pessimistic, but a first visit to Northumberland
will shock many active climbers. The standard of soloing here is incredibly high, and this is encouraged by a strict code of practice: top-roping is
frowned on due to the potential erosion at the tops of the crags.

Consequently routes are normally attempted on sight. Add to this the fact that many of the lines are fairly devoid of protection and you soon see why most visitors drop a handful of grades when they come to Northumberland. The rewards for this bold approach are worth while though: beautiful places with short but immensely satisfying routes.

The only time when this goes wrong is when routes are undergraded. It is very important here, more than elsewhere, to be cautious about the grades given to routes. Despite the fact that each edition of the guide-book has upped many routes, there are still some very nasty sandbags – routes which appear up to two grades out from a national standard. This is partially accounted for by the style of climbing, which requires some getting used to, but it is also a reflection of the isolation of the county from the mainstream of British climbing. In fact, climbing in the county has been dominated by a very small group of people for over 20 years. It is not surprising that the routes chosen here – along with virtually every other classic in Northumberland – were first climbed by the most active members of that group, John Earl and Bob Smith. Having somebody local around to give you some tips can be very advantageous – jokes about accent aside!

The general principle I have always adopted is to ignore the grade and climb for as high as I can still reverse every move or jump off. At least once this has led to spectacular problems: it is amazing how little height there is between where you are prepared to jump off and where you are not! These are the moments when you really have to tighten your stomach and either attempt that parachute roll you once saw on television or concentrate hard, take a deep breath and climb on.

On this occasion two of us had been bouldering out the start to an E4 6a arête. Clearly, the start was 6a, and the landing was not ideal, some boulders mixed into a heathery slope. We both felt that it would be safe to jump from the small ledge at 12 feet that seemed to signify the end of the difficulties, but we were having a frustrating time reaching it. Eventually, after a couple of uncomfortable landings, I made it to the ledge, only to feel that I really didn't want to jump. Reversing was not on; any jump would need to be controlled because of the landing, and as the upper arête had not looked too bad, I decided to carry on. I carefully picked my way up a further 15 feet or so of 5b climbing to reach what had looked like a good break. It wasn't; even worse, it was very sandy. I was starting to feel a little weak, and a sudden rush of fear seemed to accelerate this. I pulled up and put my right foot on a small foothold about a foot below the break. I thought if I stood up on that I would reach the top, so gently I pushed down with my arms. When my arms were fully extended. I realized that I couldn't actually take a hand off and, worse, because the break was so poor I couldn't reverse that move either. Despite encouragement from my friend that the top was good, I had no idea what to do. Slowly, I started to panic, remembering those boulders below; remembering, too, a previous occasion when I had fallen from about this height and spent three months on my back in hospital. Then I had reached a no-go situation like this and just wobbled until I fell. Determined now at least to try something, I hooked my left toe around the arête to hold me in balance for as long as possible and threw both hands up towards the top; both held, though my right foot shot off, and I rolled over the top a trembling mass of jelly. I'm sure that was the difficult variation but E5 6b would have been nearer the mark!

Despite this, Northumberland keeps pulling me back. It is a thrilling place to climb. Many of the crags can be visited in combinations if you are paying a flying visit. If you are prepared to keep well within your grade and enjoy climbing without a rope, then Bowden combined with Kyloe-in-the-Wood makes for a day of contrasting atmosphere – the latter offering more opportunity to get the rope out but feeling slightly more remote than Bowden. It is easy enough to notch up a couple of dozen quality routes right across the grades. Sandy Crag is something altogether different though.

To begin with, it is a real effort just to get there. The approach is not obvious, the crag being invisible until the later stages. Park at the picnic site on the B6341, two miles south of Hepple. Follow the road south for about 200 yards to a sharp right on a bridge. Follow the track that goes straight on for three-quarters of a mile to Midgey Ha, a cottage. Cross the stream and follow a track up left through the heather. In late August the heather is laden with pollen, and you can quite literally get dusted from head to toe. As the distinctive double horizontal breaks at the top of the crag become visible, the going gets tougher, with deep holes and sharp boulders hidden like gamekeeper's traps.

All three of the routes described start near a noticeable shallow cave at the right-hand end, above a solitary patch of grass. Sandy Crack is the compellingly obvious crack-line beginning in the cave; Greenford Road takes the holdless groove on the right arête; and Angel Fingers is the slim finger crack running the full height of the buttress to the left of the Vertical Vice, the chimney left of Sandy Crack.

Sandy Crack is a beautifully proportioned climb of contrasts. Perfectly protectable yet requiring commitment, the wrong width but requiring elegant climbing, it first shocks you, then seduces you. The initial bulge is like some 1950s Whillans' route, powerful but irritatingly awkward at the same time; getting wedged in the bulge is no more difficult than getting out of that position, so fight it and don't give up. Your reward is above, a perfect hand crack in a slab. Unfortunately, it is only perfect for a few feet, as the crack tapers towards its top and the slab steepens considerably as the crack narrows. Fortunately, Friends provide good protection – except that they become very difficult to place the higher you go. This probably sounds demoralizing; you very quickly realize that the last few feet of the crack are going to provide the crux, and that the keys to success are commitment, rapid movement and determination. The climbing above is easier but still absorbing, balancing the start.

Being the most obvious line at the crag, it is natural to go for Sandy Crack first. Although much easier, many climbers will find it a better proposition than Angel Fingers, which has an even more ferocious start. There is nothing worse than hiking miles up to some desolate but recommended crag and then failing miserably to get off the ground on the first route. Many 5b leaders (and not a few above that!) would have that experience if they started on Angel Fingers, which is a shame; the climbing above is sensational and yet protectable and on good holds throughout. If you can fathom out the initial moves, and you can commit yourself to doing them, the easier climbing above is especially delightful.

On my last visit here I couldn't resist a look at what is probably the most interesting feature: the shallow corner groove to the right of Sandy Crack. It is a clean line, but obviously sees very little traffic, so I arranged an abseil inspection with the excuse that the route needed a light brushing – a rag is normally sufficient. If a closer look doesn't leave you disheartened, then you are either brave or foolish; there are few holds, and even less opportunities for protection. The route starts by traversing out from Sandy Crack, and most leaders will place suitably high Friends before beginning this. The traverse becomes increasingly difficult, and at its end there is a steep stretch of rock up to good holds. The moves up are obvious and clean technique, safe in the knowledge that you will only swing a bit if you fail, makes them seem reasonable, although they are probably technically the hardest. Soon, you are at the foot of the groove proper, and those Friends are horizontally a long way away. Worse, the groove is blank, and what to do next is not clear-cut.

The secret is to climb on your feet and trust your sense of balance. Although precarious, the second crux is soon over, and then a good hold and a potential runner placement calms your butterflies before the still tricky romp up the final section. Give your second a little slack in the groove, so he can get the most from the experience!

You could easily be convinced, particularly at Back Bowden Doors, that Northumberland climbing is all about power and dynamic fluid movements. Much of it is; but like climbing on its cousins, the gritstones of Yorkshire and Derbyshire, there are also times when the sandstone of Northumberland requires the subtlety of slow precise movements. Greenford Road is an excellent example of this subtlety.

LAKE DISTRICT

Borrowdale

- **■ LOCATION •** Reecastle Crag, two and a half miles up the Watendlath road which branches off the main Borrowdale road two miles south of Keswick.

- **■ ROUTES •** White Noise (E3 5c), Penal Servitude (E5 6b).

- **■ FIRST ASCENTS •** White Noise – Jeff Lamb, Ray McHaffie (1978); Penal Servitude – Dave Armstrong, Pete Whillance (1981).

- **■ CONSIDERATIONS •** Reecastle is only a short walk from the road, and it is a popular crag on summer evenings. The Watendlath road is easily blocked, so park carefully.

- **■ GUIDEBOOK •** *Borrowdale* by R. Kenyon (Fell and Rock Climbing Club, 1990).

REECASTLE HAS become something of a nationally important crag over the last few years, receiving attention from a considerable number of visiting climbers. Being only a small crag, with 25 or so routes, and in the same valley as Goat Crag and Shepherd's Crag, it might be worth thinking through why this is so. It could be seen as an example of what a bit of publicity can do for a crag: a couple of articles in the climbing Press and another crowded and spoiled crag, rubbish lapping at its feet, is born. I reject that idea though, because there are also heavily publicized crags for whom publicity is no catapult to popularity.

I suspect it has more to do with the prevailing mood among climbers when the publicity arrives. Crags come into and go out of vogue, and the reasons for this are often simple: among them, the grades and quality of their routes, accessibility, and proximity to other areas. Craig-y-Forwen in North Wales went from being a quiet little backwater to a nationally important crag in a matter of months, following the publication of a new guidebook; soon its foot was littered with rubbish, the road beneath was blocked with cars and, subsequently, access has been lost to everyone. Craig-y-Forwen had a good range of routes, with classics in most grades from VS upwards; the climbing was relatively short, with excellent protection; the access was easy, a few minutes from the road; it was on the way to and from North Wales for many people, and, lastly, it enjoyed better weather than the mountains. For all these reasons it was bound to become popular: it was exactly what people were looking for at a time of increasing interest in steep limestone, short pitches and easy access.

I was fortunate to be one of the few English climbers who visited Buoux, in the south of France, before 1983. It was an amazingly quiet place, with very few climbers even at the weekends. Some French climbers were sleeping beneath the crags, and we were lucky in finding somebody in the village (an alpinist of Rebuffat's generation) whose interest in climbing prompted him to put us up. There were few bolts in the rock, and a recent campaign had been waged against the use of fixed pegs! Returning a year later, having heard about the problems that had arisen at Easter, I was depressed at how quickly the atmosphere had changed. Something special had been spoilt by what boiled down to a massive influx of visitors; yet the publicity in England and Spain had not led to this, apart from feeding a need at that time.

With the massive increase in numbers of climbers looking for short hard climbs, especially safe ones, that has characterized the late 1980s and early 1990s, it is not surprising that a little publicity for Reecastle has led to a massive rise in the numbers visiting the crag. The access is easy, being only five minutes' level stroll from the car; it gets the afternoon sun; and although small, has a collection of excellent climbs in the Extreme grades. For anyone who enjoys the prospect of climbing steep and essentially safe rock, with the spectacular Lake District scenery as a backdrop, it is an obvious choice; not necessarily better than many of its near neighbours in Borrowdale, but in many ways easier. This is the age of putting convenience first.

This is not to say that Reecastle has been spoilt, yet. It is still possible to be alone there (though probably not at weekends), and I have no doubt that the atmosphere of Watendlath is at its most enjoyable when that is so. It is always possible to seek out quiet times for busy crags, and in this case desirable to do so. The first visit I made was one summer evening in the week, trying to snatch a few hours at the end of the journey up to the Lakes. Driving up the delightful little road to Watendlath after the nausea of the M6 and A66 was just what was needed to relax the mind and widen the eyes. Each curve in the road brings something new into view, and it is hard not to be excited when the crag appears on the left-hand side. We walked slowly, savouring the stillness of the air, and enjoying the shadows that the hills were already throwing across the valley. Another team arrived not long after us, but being locals who were content to avoid the obvious routes that we wanted to do, the essential peace of the place remained intact.

White Noise is one of the most obvious lines, and, being pictured in our guidebook we had to do it first. This part of the crag is barrel shaped, with a very bulging lower wall easing round to an easy angled slab in its 100-foot height. White Noise takes the blatant leftwards-leading crack-line that starts about 20 feet up, just left of the central fault of the Rack. Tossing a coin established that it was my lead, and I quickly geared up. In common with many of the other routes, the start is actually quite committing, though a cunningly placed wire between two shallow flakes and a flexible half Friend made me feel happier. Steep moves on very positive holds lead up and leftwards quickly to a brilliant hand jam, and bomb-proof runners where the angle starts to ease. From here, the moves are just superb, with big holds, deep pockets and positive flakes following the crack-line up on to the slab where the angle eases. Protection is excellent, and if you anticipate doing another route, you can easily rig a belay and abseil off from the top (a couple of long slings will make pulling the ropes down much easier).

Abseiling down from the top of White Noise, it's possible to sneak a quick look at Penal Servitude. This takes the wall to the left of White Noise, past a very obvious peg jutting out from a break low down. The upper wall looked easy enough, with a liberal sprinkling of good flakes and an easy angle, but the section just past the peg looked hard. A small set of layaways up and right from the peg were very heavily chalked, and among them was a nut slot that had clearly seen more than enough action. I opted to check the runner placement, even though the locals told me that it was an RP 2. I managed to get three different runners in the slot, but none of them were that inspiring. I settled on the RP 2 on the basis that it had worked for others, and slid down to the ground.

Time was getting on, so a quick sort out of gear and away. The start involves some thuggy pulls on only fair holds until the sanctuary of the break with the peg is reached. Spending too long working out which holds to use, and trying in vain to place a couple of runners, I only just got to the peg first go, and didn't even try the moves above before sagging on to the rope and coming back down. I was completely pumped – after only 15 feet! I asked Andy if he wanted a go while I rested, but he was happy to sit around at the bottom and enjoy the last bit of sunlight. I wanted to rest properly, but there wasn't really time, so after about five minutes I psyched up again and shook my arms thoroughly in an attempt to look determined. Up more easily this time, avoiding a tricky hand change by stretching past one of the holds, and quickly I was by the peg. Chalk up, put the RP 2 and quickdraw in my mouth, throw a foot up and start pushing: I quickly snatched my right hand on to the lowest of the layaways – it held. Adjusting my feet slightly I started to pull up, out of balance, and before I could find a suitable pocket for my left hand, the fingers on my right hand uncurled and I was off. I spat the useless RP out from between my teeth, and returned to the ground once more. The locals were laughing, in a friendly way: 'Hard, isn't it?'

I decided to forget the RP. I knew there was a large Rock placement some 12 feet up and left from the peg, at the first big hold, and I felt that I needed to do it quickly if I was to do it at all. The shadows were lengthening at an alarming rate now, and the local team was packing to go. 'Having another go, are you? We'll see you in the pub, then.' Andy nodded vigorously, probably wishing he was going with them.

'I'll just have one more go,' I told him, though he picked up the doubt in my voice.

'No problem, take your time; you can do it.'

It went quiet for a few minutes, and then I got up, swinging my arms again, scratching at the insects that had started to emerge, squeaking my boots. 'Right,' and with a few deep breaths I was off again. The pulls up to the peg felt like a ladder, and I had time to think. Once again I rocked up and snatched the layaway, but this time I steadied myself, pushed again and snatched higher. My fingers caught the very top layaway and my thumb hooked over a small edge as well. I left my right foot alone and, with the added grip from the thumb, leant out slightly and brought my left foot up, outside edge, and started pushing. There were pockets everywhere, most of them chalked, but I felt in balance and probed two or three before my left hand hooked a sharp edge. I was amazed at how strong I felt as I stood up and reached through with my right. I soon found a good pocket. Burying the tip of my toe out left in a further pocket, I rocked up leftwards and, although it felt harder, I soon had the jug. I struggled a little to find the big Rock on my harness, but the outcome was not in doubt then, and as the angle eased I enjoyed the feeling of success. The upper section was bold but straightforward, and the belay was soon in hand.

'Are you following?' I called down, but I had had my goodwill for the night, and before I looked down Andy began packing up. I abseiled for the runners, while Andy walked round for the belay, and we were soon walking back to the car, almost hidden in the dark. We found the locals in the pub, and I was smug with myself for having managed the route.

'Of course, you had looked at it on the rope,' one of them said, poking fun. Perhaps that is why Reecastle is a modern crag. I had certainly taken a modern approach to it, pre-inspection and testing runners. 'Do you think you could redpoint it now?' he asked, and I laughed at the thought. 'Loads of people leave all the runners in and redpoint it, you know.' Somehow it seems funny to treat that route like a sport route, but in the absence of anything closer hereabouts, perhaps that is what has happened. Yo-yoing to the high point almost seems traditional in comparison, and I joked about wanting to copy the style of the first ascent.

The next time I went to Reecastle, there were 16 people there, with cars parked very badly along the road, and three leaders climbed Penal Servitude with all the runners in. It spoilt it for me, like my second visit to Buoux. I wonder if people have just turned Reecastle into a modern crag because of its hard routes, and I wonder how long it will be before the unnecessary intrusion of bolts will tarnish this piece of rock. Have we not learnt from the messes we have made in the past? Reecastle deserves popularity, but we need to show some environmental awareness if we are to avoid turning it into the climbing dustbin of Borrowdale.

Southern Lakes

■ **LOCATION** • Hodge Close Quarry, reached by following a signposted minor road from the A593 two miles north of Coniston. Chapel Head Scar is above Witherslack Hall, two miles north of the A590. Take the Witherslack turning and keep going until the Hall is reached on a sharp bend.

■ **ROUTES** • Ten Years After (E4 5c), Moonchild/Lunatic (E4 5c), Android (E4 5c).

■ **FIRST ASCENTS** • Ten Years After – Rob Matheson, Ed Cleasby (1980); Moonchild/Lunatic – Ron Fawcett, Al Parker, Dave Parker (1974), and Pete Livesey, John Sheard (1974); Android – Ed Cleasby, with some aid (1978), later freed by Dave Knighton (1980).

■ **CONSIDERATIONS** • Hodge Close is a very quick-drying crag, though very unpleasant in the wrong conditions. Chapel Head Scar is subject to a bird ban of varying lengths, but normally from 1 March to 31 July.

■ **GUIDEBOOKS** • *Scafell, Dow and Eskdale* by A. Phizacklea (Fell and Rock Climbing Club, 1988); *Rock Climbs – Lancashire and the North West* by Phil Kelly and Dave Cronshaw (Cicerone, 1989). A *Lake District RockFax* is due in 1994.

THE LAKE District has so much climbing to offer that it is almost impossible to pick out the best places I have visited, or the most enjoyable climbs I have done. Pillar Rock on a weekday summer evening is difficult to beat, and a contender for one of the best days out I have ever had started by climbing Ichabod on the east buttress of Scafell at eight in the morning and being too hot in a T-shirt.

Having begun walking, and then climbing, in the Lake District, it is natural that I feel especially fond of certain little nooks and crannies in the mountains. There are also some superb valley crags here though, and the south Lakes in particular are blessed with a number of excellent venues that have plenty of interest in their own right.

One of the most interesting venues is Hodge Close Quarry, a very unusual place, seemingly at odds with its mountainous surroundings, for to climb here you must first go down. Easily found down a long and narrow road that breaks off from the main Coniston to Ambleside road, Hodge Close is the sort of quarry that should never have come into existence in the middle of the Lake District. It is ultimately an ugly place, a deep hole in the ground with a murky pool at the bottom, and the remnants of much of the quarrying business all too evident. Yet in the right light of an autumn evening, particularly when nobody else is there, it can be as fine a place as most quarries, and somehow the climbing there can seem particularly challenging.

Originally developed with a minimal use of fixed gear, there are a number of excellent test-pieces up the steep slate slabs above the pool. Modern routes have appeared with copious bolts, and the neighbouring Parrock Quarry has become a veritable sports climbing arena, boasting numerous short, safe, forgettable exercises. However, it is the older routes that provide the most interest here, and Ten Years After is as good as they come.

A purist approach will involve abseiling either well to the side of the route, which is quite simple to arrange, or descending into the adjacent Parrock Quarry, which is easily found just beyond Hodge Close, and then coming into the bowels of Hodge Close itself through the convenient archway. The bottom of this hole is quite fascinating, and well worth a bit of exploring: occasionally you find divers disappearing into the inky depths, presumably to salvage what they can from any of a number of badly parked cars below. Once you have satisfied your curiosity and got your bearings, you can think about climbing again and head over to the foot of Ten Years After. This is reached by some precarious boulder hopping and a short but fairly unpleasant 4c corner past more relics of the quarry's former life.

Once established on the large ledge next to the big overhang beneath Ten Years After, you can start forgetting about the place and think about the climbing. Originally graded E3, this is the sort of route that can really throw people, being quite bold and sustained, with only a handful of runners in nearly a full rope length. The crux, fortunately, is low down and near to two of those runners; an easy flake starts the route, but you soon leave that for the less obvious wall to the left. A peg runner, and a good nut to the right, mark the start of the crux. It's the sort of climbing you would do instantly on the ground, but already you feel part of a serious venture, and I have seen one party spend nearly an hour over the next few feet. To their credit though, they eventually climbed on, and once you do, a feast of brilliant climbing is laid before you. All at a steady 5a/b, with the odd reachier move probably notching 5c for the shorter climber, the rest of the slab slowly unfolds, with very little runner placing to interrupt the concentration!

Sitting on the edge of the quarry, you don't really have the panoramic views you associate with the Lake District, but there are times when the quality of the climbing compensates for that, and the atmosphere at Hodge Close is unusual enough to make even that a bonus. Coming there after a day on Dow Crag, just for a quick route of a summer's evening, is the perfect way to spend a flying visit to the south Lakes.

By contrast Chapel Head Scar is a fine setting. Although the walk in is very short, it is still possible to feel that you are in the Lake District. Again, this is not the clichéd image of the Lake District, but the Witherslack Valley has some charm, and the peace is more real than at many more famous Lake District venues. It is not unusual to hear little more than a woodpecker all day at this impressive crag.

The Great Buttress at Chapel Head Scar is aptly named, its steepness and perfect rock making it the show-piece of the south Lakes valley crags. The numerous tufa pillars provide some excellent holds, and the quality of the rock generally is quite exceptional. Getting the bulk of any available sunshine and suffering from only slight patches of seepage, the fact that the bird ban limits climbing to the autumn and winter months is no problem at all. Many of the routes are excellent, most of the rest are good, and nearly all employ bolt protection. Right in the middle of the buttress, however, is a traditional route of immense character and beauty – Android.

On first sight, the glaring difficulty in climbing any route on the buttress is going to be breaching the first 30 feet, where the rock is steepest. There are some very hard solutions to this problem, some of which are on the most painful crozzly rock I have come across, but the solution provided by Android is one that any self-respecting adventurer would be proud of: you climb a tree. It's fun because the tree is not sturdy, overhangs as dramatically as the rock, and it's not very tall, so you end up standing on the highest branches. Fortunately, it is easy enough to clip one of the ropes into a bolt that protects the free climb For When the Tree Goes up the adjacent rock, but it is still quite scary gaining a standing position on the topmost branch. One day the tree will go, the damage of numerous hands and boots on its branches having already stripped it to a dying skeleton of a specimen, so the succour of a sling runner round the tree itself is of little real consequence. Once stood on the top of the tree, you can clip a bolt on the wall itself and start contemplating the real climbing.

Android is graded E4 5c, and the climbing itself is never that hard, but it is always committing and exciting, and leaving the tree is no exception. Finding the best holds, which are all small, you must commit yourself to bouncing on to the rock, from where there will be no return. A quick pull gains a flat hold, using this confidently finds a better one above and you can soon rock up into the first of many resting positions on the route.

Take in your surroundings: you have made three moves and are already 35 feet up and some ten feet out from the base of the rock! A horizontal ledge system runs intermittently leftwards from your feet, so you head leftwards carefully into better handholds and a curious tied-off, double-peg affair that counts for a runner. Now left again, slightly lower and with a tricky finger change on a small positive hold, until a good layaway provides some relaxation beneath a very sturdy-looking peg.

The next 20 feet are intimidating but probably no more than 5a. Good flake holds, the odd small wire and reasonable rests lead up the wall to a superb position where the flake system runs out. Here, fortunately, you can place excellent wires, for the next section is both committing and hard; a large hanging flake high up and right is the next protection, so concentrate and don't fall off.

Unusually for such a steep crag, the problem is one of balance rather than brawn. After bridging up a few moves, an obvious step right beckons, the exact choice of handholds providing the difficulty. Once you have stepped right, the enormous layaway you would reasonably expect after such a crux fails to appear, but the climbing is still in balance, so hold on and teeter round the arête until, at last, a positive hold can be firmly gripped.

Easier now, but all the time leaving those runners behind, you can climb up to the flake and good runners, then a short but fun layback finishes the route off. The well-endowed belay six feet right of the top of the flake avoids some nasty rock higher up, and if you have managed your ropes carefully, you will be able to lower off and enjoy your second's antics on the tree from below.

Standing well down the slope belaying Paul as he seconded the route, I was struck more than before by the scale of the buttress, and by the superb way in which Android navigates the easiest way up this wall. There is something classical about its approach, and I sincerely hope routes like this will continue to evade the pillage of the bolt drill so that future generations, who will no doubt all enjoy the many bolted routes on the buttress, can experience this more historical approach for themselves.

In many ways it is not surprising that among the many other fine climbs at Chapel Head Scar, and there are many, the other route that so clearly sticks in my mind is also one with a classical pedigree, Moonchild, a Ron Fawcett creation. It has some brilliant climbing above a very committing start, and because (unlike the more modern routes) you can't cheat your way up it, it is rarely attempted. The climbing is superb though, and it is more than worth making the effort to psyche up for the start.

The route follows the groove-line in the right hand arête of the buttress, directly above the approach path. The problem with the start is easy to see from the ground. At about 20 feet is a peg runner, the first runner! It is possible to fiddle in a large Rock sideways in a pocket below, but it is very poor and wastes strength. The best approach is a determined 'it's only 5c' fighting stance, followed by some rapid action. The initial layaways are steep but soon you are rewarded with some very positive handholds. Just keep your feet up and you will quickly reach the peg and a decent rest. It really is 'only 5c', and there are harder starts on routes of E2 or so, but the adrenalin is really flowing by the time you reach that peg.

More relaxed now, but with some trickier climbing, you can work your way up and right, then past a further peg over a bulge to the sanctuary of easier ground and a tree belay. The first time I did Moonchild it was graded E3 5c and it felt more like E4 6a, so it was quite a shock to the system. With a compromise E4 5c in my head the second time, it didn't seem so hard, but do make sure you are feeling good.

From the tree belay you can descend or, if inspired, add to the pleasure by taking in the top, and best, pitch of Lunatic, one of Pete Livesey's routes, to give a Fawcett/Livesey outing of immense character. This involves a short traverse across and up to a good ledge and tree belay beneath an excellent-looking groove in the sweep of rock above the Great Gully. Only 40 feet long and still only 5c, this provides a brilliant continuation to the traditional style of Moonchild, and even leads you to the top, a rare experience on this crag. The descent can be made by carefully going over the top of Great Buttress and then following a good path down the steep hillside.

Once you have done these, there are plenty of superb bolt-protected routes to go at, and the crag really comes into its own with routes like Wargames and Phantom Zone, but as soon as you get on those, you don't feel in the Lake District any more.

LANCASHIRE

■ **LOCATION** • Trowbarrow Quarry, about three quarters of a mile south-east of Silverdale railway station, on the Silverdale to Yealand Redmayne road; ten minutes from Junction 35 on the M6. Hoghton Quarry, deep in the woods near Hoghton Tower, just off the A675 Blackburn to Preston road.

■ **ROUTES** • Cracked Actor (E2 5b), Mandarin (E2 5b), Rhododendron Arête (E3 6a), Doubting Thomas (E5 6b), All Roads Lead to Rome (E5 6b).

■ **FIRST ASCENTS** • Cracked Actor – Al Evans (1975); Mandarin – John Hamer (1965); Rhododendron Arête – Dave Knighton, Dave Cronshaw (1979); Doubting Thomas – Dave Bates (1984); All Roads Lead to Rome – Gary Gibson (1983).

■ **CONSIDERATIONS** • The rock at Trowbarrow is clean, quick-drying, limestone, getting plenty of sun. Access is easy, but you may be asked to leave. The quarry is in the Silverdale–Arnside Area of Outstanding Natural Beauty. Hoghton is a shady gritstone quarry, often dirty due to the restricted access (climbing allowed February to June inclusive).

■ **GUIDEBOOK** • *Rock Climbs – Lancashire and the North West* by Phil Kelly and Dave Cronshaw (Cicerone, 1989).

TROWBARROW QUARRY is one of those places I had heard about for 15 years before I finally got round to going there, and even then it was almost by accident. Part of the problem is that it is so close to the Lake District that you can easily find yourself driving past it and never taking the trouble to find out where it is.

In fact, this is a bit of a problem with Lancashire generally! It is so easy to think of crags in the more glamorous Yorkshire Dales, and fail to appreciate the immense wealth of climbing near by that has been kept out of the public eye. I can vaguely remember a few people raving about Hoghton, and seeing a slide of Gary Gibson on All Roads Lead to Rome, in a brief burst of publicity in 1983; even so, I suspect Lancashire cliffs remained untouched by most outsiders for many years.

This is exactly the sort of situation an excellent new guidebook can remedy, and when the 1989 Lancashire guidebook came out of my Christmas stocking, I had little idea what a valuable present it would be. Having got into the habit many years ago of always carrying at least six unnecessary guidebooks in the car when I go anywhere (so I can wish I was somewhere else when it rains), I found myself driving over to Lancashire from a wet and busy Malham campsite one Sunday morning, with a sceptical passenger. Neither of us really believed the generous quantity of stars the guidebook dished out to Trowbarrow to be accurate, and as we were going further away from home on a wet day, there was a good chance of being miserable if our gamble didn't pay off.

As it turned out, the guidebook's encouraging comments about a favourable microclimate proved accurate, and the sun appeared at the same time as the M6. The area that surrounds Trowbarrow is much more scenic than might be imagined, and by the time we left the car in a muddy parking space and stepped into the silvery woods, we were already feeling optimistic about the place. Arriving a few minutes later in the quarry, small but open and full of sun, it was difficult to contain our excitement. By the time we left, many hours later, we had 20 routes under our belts, including bagfuls of stars, had been undisturbed all day, and Trowbarrow had become a regular stop-off fixture on the way back from the Lakes.

A warning though: there may come a time when there is no point in going there! The quarry is technically still being worked, and it is per-fectly possible that the owners will one day decide to remove the best rock for their own purposes. Indeed Main Wall – the most noticeable sweep of limestone on the right as you enter the quarry – only appeared thanks to the quarrymen in 1970. Its huge cracked features provide sev-eral distinct lines, all of which are good. The stars are scattered fairly lib-erally, and reasonably accurately, with top honours going to Jean Jeanie and Cracked Actor by a narrow margin. It is with some regret that I pass over Aladdinsane, the most obvious line, but although a personal favourite, this fearsome wide crack has not proved endearingly popular among the suitors I have taken to Trowbarrow. The noble art of leg wedging is still alive (and kicking!) but not revered: cult material only, perhaps … Jean Jeanie takes the obvious rightwards-rising stepped crack-line right of Aladdinsane. It is as fine a crack pitch as any in the country, with more than enough bite for its VS grade.The secret is to relax and try to keep as much body out of the crack as possible (as opposed to Aladdinsane …).

The Main Wall is home to a number of other excellent climbs – Hollow Earth (HVS) and Harijan (VS) should be on any climber's tick list. But the climbing on these routes is similar to Jean Jeanie, and it is with a step up in grades that the next best route appears. Cracked Actor is a brilliant E2 pitch up the wall to the left of Jean Jeanie, starting beneath Aladdinsane but breaking out left up the thin crack-line. The moves up this are sustained, but excellent jams are available, and the protection is superb. Although only really a short route, it epitomizes the E2 5b grade for this type of limestone route – sustained but safe. All the difficulties are concentrated into the first 25 feet of the thin crack; make it that far and you are rewarded with huge jugs leading up leftwards to the top. There is an added bonus in the large number of comfortable spectator blocks on the quarry floor below, so take the family and a picnic, and you should climb with style.

Elsewhere in the quarry there are three other walls of good rock, and a large amount of rubbish. Left from Main Wall is the crozzly slab of Asylum Wall. This and the Red Wall hidden in the trees opposite provide contrasting high-grade exercises, both with some hard and sometimes bold pitches. The Red Wall is a popular training venue, and stays dry in light rain. Although the climbing on both sections is consistently difficult, both walls have negative factors: Asylum wall is a touch friable for its generally bold routes, and the Red Wall is prone to greasiness. However, the most interesting piece of rock is further in the quarry beyond Asylum Wall.

Assagai Wall is easily recognized by its striking fluted upper section, where natural weathering has resulted in a series of beautifully smooth grooves. The lower section is quarried though, and the combination of technical slab climbing on tiny holds on the quarried lower section followed by varied climbing on interesting natural holds above, makes Doubting Thomas a classic. The lower section is incredibly bold too, so the easier climbing above the bulge feels well deserved. The move through the bulge is brilliant; just do it and see.

Having been surprised and impressed by Trowbarrow, I soon started a bit of a campaign to visit all the Lancashire crags and to get to know the county better. Time after time I came back from days full of enthusiasm, just amazed that the climbing Press had advertised the place so little. There were bad days, but I'll let you find those out for yourself! The main advantage of the area is that, as in the Peak District, it is very easy to move from crag to crag. On one occasion I was at Anglezarke, the one crag that seems to be truly popular here, and getting very annoyed with the hot, sweaty atmosphere and the numerous non-climbing noisies playing their stereos. A quick flick through the guide, a memory of old conversations and that photo, and we were heading to Hoghton.

Now, it has to be said that Hoghton is a funny place. In scale it compares to the likes of Millstone, with pitches of up to 130 feet long. It doesn't have the quantity of rock of Millstone, though, and it is unusual for a quarry in that climbing is restricted to between February and June inclusive: the quarry is actually part of a breeding-ground for gamebirds. In addition, there are a substantial number of trees that don't help the mainly north-facing walls dry out after the winter. Is your mouth watering yet?

One route that does get a reasonable amount of traffic, judging by its normally clean state, is Mandarin, an excellent introduction to the quarry. As you enter the quarry, the first section of crag is known as Hoghton Wall, which actually consists of two walls at right angles. The right-hand wall is steep and looks friable, but left of the corner is a fine stretch of rock, invariably bright green with lichen, which provides the longest routes here. The wall is generally just off vertical, although towards its left edge substantial roofs appear. Mandarin takes a line up the left edge and works its way through the most impressive roofs, and is always lichen free.

One year I climbed Mandarin in the middle of March. Apart from a few dabs of chalk on a short bolt route at the left end of an amazing unclimbed wall, the quarry was in as unfriendly looking a state imaginable. Every wall was glowing with the rich green of semi-dry lichen, and it seemed barely believable that routes like Boadicea (a classic E2) had ever been climbed, let alone recently. We were alone, and suddenly – at exactly the same time – we both suggested climbing chalk free all day, to leave the crag looking unvisited. It was settled, and we quickly prepared to climb. Mandarin is described in the guidebook as two pitches, and the first pitch looks very amenable for its 5b grade.

Do not be deceived: the short slab at the start tricks the eye, and as soon as you reach the two broken-off carving knives that serve for 'metal spikes' and look up, you will appreciate the nature of the rock above. A little higher, a good peg (adjacent to an appalling one – a feature of Hoghton) on the right can be clipped. Boldly, but fairly easily, swing out right and pull up on to a flake. A quick layback up the edge of this gains a bridging position beneath a roof, and thankfully at last some good runners. Moving round the roof is easier than it looks, and quickly you are stood on a sloping shelf above. A Friend 3.5 or 4 helps protect the next moves, the crux, although neither are essential. The moves after them require a cunning bit of bridging, or use of a crafty undercut. In essence, they are balance moves, but that seems strange in such an overhung groove. Don't snatch the top of the little arête either, as it is not as flat as it could be. At this point I placed a good wire, clipped one of the pegs and dutifully bridged, chimneyed and laybacked out left and up to a belay on the Pasture, as the large ledge is known.

On being joined by my second, however, there was clearly a problem. Neither of us particularly fancied reversing the last few moves back to the top of the groove, and the rope drag once you started to climb up again would surely be phenomenal. Quite relieved, we opted to abseil off, and return to climb it in one pitch. We had both been a little psyched out by the climbing on that first pitch, and had not really adjusted to being in this sunless place on a March day, without chalk!

The return a few months later was a different story. Some of the green had been beaten back and Mandarin was fully chalked. Climbing in one pitch, I soon got established beneath the big roof, and stepping up and right, quickly scampered out to the hanging groove above. The positions here are exceptional, and it is very fortunate that good runners can be arranged easily. Some more bridging leads to a final bulge and a tricky move up right into an even more exposed niche. Fortunately easy rock is just round the arête to the left, and the top is soon reached. Mandarin is a stunning example of how reasonable technical difficulty can take you into wild positions, and it deserves to become a national classic.

There are many other excellent routes here. The brilliant Rhododendron Buttress, climbable in its lichen coat, is very worth while, and the right arête of that buttress, Rhododendron Arête, is a superb test of will-power at E3 6a. Although it looks very blank from below, there are actually some quite good holds up there. The difficulty is in committing yourself to them quickly enough. The protection is mostly *in situ*, with some of the strangest pegs around. Low down, there are two bizarre ring pegs, with two better pegs to clip near by, and above the bolt (next to an older bolt, of course) the bold upper section is protected by a peg that must originally have been at least six inches long, as five and a half stick out from the rock! Taking a bunch of smallish wires, there is sufficient gear, and the upper arête is a lovely piece of climbing.

Sadly, there don't seem to be enough people interested in climbing at Hoghton to keep any of the harder routes clean, and our desire to see what Gibson's All Roads Lead to Rome was really like was thwarted on my first visit by the over-abundance of lichen. The route takes a line up the green slime just left of the main corner of Hoghton wall, with a surprisingly glinting bolt runner at about 80 feet – surprising, considering the rotting state of so much of the old aid gear here. The advantage of this is you can get that pioneering feeling, particularly if you abstain from chalk.

The next time I visited I was prepared, and after repeating the nearby Boadicea, I abseiled down the route, giving the wall a cursory swipe with a wire brush. It is hard to tell whether this sort of build-up of lichen can happen over one winter; I suspect that Hoghton is just out of fashion with visitors and locals alike, which seems so odd, given the large number of excellent routes and the potential for very hard new routes. I have to admit to looking quite closely at the upper section, so I can't really say how difficult it is, just that it is a beautiful sequence of moves, with the crux helped by a good stiff pair of boots.

Completely different in outlook and atmosphere, these two quarries show how diverse climbing can be. Yet they have shown me that Lancashire is an area of both great beauty and great climbing, and that there is more to this area than you can see from a passing car.

NORTH WALES

Clwyd

- ■ **LOCATION** • Craig Arthur, high above the Eglwyseg Valley that runs due north from Llangollen. Craig Arthur is the last cliff on the superb escarpment on the right before the ford at World's End, which is signposted from Llangollen.

- ■ **ROUTES** • Digitron (E2 5b), Manikins of Horror (E3 5c), Survival of the Fastest (E4 6a), Manic Mechanic (E5 6b).

- ■ **FIRST ASCENTS** • Digitron, Manikins of Horror – Stuart Cathcart, Gerald Swindley (1973/6); Survival of the Fastest – Stuart Cathcart (1978); Manic Mechanic – John Moulding, John Codling (with rests), freed by Andy Pollitt (1984).

- ■ **CONSIDERATIONS** • Park at World's End, leave nothing in your car, and walk back through the forest on the Offa's Dyke footpath. Craig Arthur is the first crag reached (20 minutes). It is not worth attempting other approaches: there are potential access problems here.

- ■ **GUIDEBOOKS** • *Clwyd Limestone* by Stuart Cathcart (Cicerone, 1983); *Clwyd Rock*, ed. Gary Dickinson (Cicerone, 1993).

IN HIS introduction to the 1983 guidebook to *Clwyd Limestone,* Stuart Cathcart began with the following comments:

"It is inevitable that every piece of rock in the British Isles will unfortunately one day be documented in texts such as this ... pioneers will be left with nothing to find …. But … it is amazing that this range of hills and especially the splendid Eglwyseg valley has remained almost untouched, and out of hearsay for so long."

Ironically, it is Clwyd limestone itself that may well prove to be the last area that is fully documented; pioneers here still have plenty to try, and it is still amazing, ten years later, that the area remains so unfrequented. In 1983, Cathcart put it down to geographical position, being 'on the way' to Snowdonia from almost everywhere. I certainly feel that not having a large population near enough to get 'evening cragging' has hindered its development, as key pioneers to an area often live near by. Yet the area is beautiful; it has all the camping facilities that you could need; it is near the bright lights of Llangollen (or peaceful spots up at World's End for those in search of quiet), and it has literally miles of rock up to a respectable height. Furthermore, the rock is good quality limestone, generally very sound, and there are no tidal or seasonal restrictions: so why don't people climb there?

Driving up the Eglwyseg Valley from Llangollen for the first time is a sobering experience: the rock never seems to end, all of it in clear view and all looking very impressive. The strange little spot at the World's End ford is often quite busy, and indeed the crag immediately above the ford, another Craig-y-Forwen, often seems to have a handful of parties beavering away on its polished routes. There are some good routes to be had here, particularly on the obvious exposed face of the upper tier, although such accessible fare is best left for the end of the day; so head back down the valley for a few yards until a well-marked path, part of the Offa's Dyke footpath, cuts into the forest. A good path contours the hillside, and several hundred yards after emerging from the trees, the main crag of the escarpment is seen, Craig Arthur.

From this end, the cliff does not look too imposing, although as you scramble steeply up the scree the rock seems to increase in height. Once beneath the crag, the significance of Craig Arthur becomes all too apparent. With routes reaching up to almost a full rope length and some classic lines, all situated above a steep grass slope (that will take a chalk bag or misplaced training shoe a long way), it is clear that Craig Arthur is potentially as important as many Peak and Yorkshire outcrops. Indeed the comparison is a fair one, as the climbing style is not dissimilar, and the limestone itself very similar.

At the left-hand end, the short but powerful line of Le Chacal takes a good-looking corner and roof (at a strenuous E2 5c), with the easier and devious line of A Touch of Class (E2 5b) starting at the same place but heading off rightwards and up before finishing above the roofs. Both are good, but neither really gives a good introduction to the crag – the one being too strenuous, the other too scrappy. About 50 yards further on though, a good-looking groove bounds the left-hand side of a fine white arête, with a large yew tree to the right of the arête, two-thirds of the way up. Digitron (E2 5b) takes a line up this area of rock, and it is a superb introduction to Clwyd limestone, packing a good variety of rock and climbing into its rope length.

Digitron starts with a fairly bold little wall leading up rightwards to the foot of the groove; a couple of peg runners provide some reassurance, and the climbing is not particularly hard, but the hollowness of a couple of the holds is a little unnerving. Soon, good holds and fine rock lead up a crack-line to a depression beneath a small roof. The next few moves are hard direct, but a sneaky move out left and then back right is possible a few feet higher. Either way, the lip of the bulge is gained, and a swing round the arête made on to a thin footledge that leads easily rightwards into the arms of the yew tree. It is possible to belay in the tree, but better, if you feel up to it, to continue to the top. A steep move leads up, just left of the tree, to a horizontal break, and a rockover leftwards to gain good holds. Once above the bulge, the final slab looks disarmingly hard, with a particularly blank section at the top. Have faith: climb the thin crack to its end and then give everything you've got to reach up high on the right for a good hidden pocket, and it is soon over. As you sit on the rabbit-cropped turf atop the cliff, you can watch the walkers traversing the hillside below and enjoy the peace of having a crag to yourself.

An easy descent – just above where the path up through the scree meets the crag – soon gets you back to the bottom, and just to the left of Digitron you can get ready for the harder routes on Manikins of Horror. This route starts just right of a yew tree at the foot of the crag, at a shallow cave. Just right of the cave, climb easily, but again with a little care, up to the horizontal break, and then more confidently step left and up into a corner with a peg runner. The next section is tricky, so make sure you are happy with your gear before bridging up slightly before pulling out leftwards and around the arête on to a very smooth slab, and a good rest. Above is a small overlap, with a steep crack rising above it. Numerous pegs provide adequate protection for the next 20 feet, and it is well worth relying on them and climbing reasonably quickly. A thin step up to the overlap is followed by a series of increasingly strenuous pulls, all on good holds, until the horizontal break is reached. Here, you've got to use your feet well, as the jugs run out and a long reach needs to be made up to a good fingerhold. It is a very steep position, but get your right foot up high and commit yourself to upward movement; once stood in the break, everything feels more relaxed. A short wall, easier angled now, leads up to a small tree, and then easier climbing leads to the top. Many people will probably agree with the E2 5c grade in the old guide, but I feel that Manikins just makes it into the E3 category, being quite strenuous and sustained.

Like many limestone cliffs, the very best routes along the whole escarpment are to be found in the upper Extreme grades. When the 1983 guide came out, the E5 category had been barely scratched in this area, with an enigmatic and unique number grade replacing the adjectival grade for the shorter crags, obscuring even the odd real E5 anyway! However, at the time the hardest route in the obligatory 'graded list' was a route called Survival of the Fastest. This was, undoubtedly, also one of the very best routes in the guide, and it was also unusual in that it featured a protection bolt.

Walking back along the base of the crag beneath Manikins of Horror and past the foot of Digitron, you eventually come to a very impressive section of rock, the Nemesis wall. This sheet of limestone is broken by a spectacular curving crack in its left-hand side, the line of Survival of the Fastest.

The climbing on this route is as difficult as the route is obvious. The mandatory careful start gains a ledge below the crack-line proper, which leans away slightly to the right. A committing move gains the start of the crack, and some swift pulls lead quickly to a reasonable rest. The crux follows: no single move is outrageous, although a few are very sequency, and the fact that the holds will not be chalked up most of the time will not help weaker parties. However, for move after move, a powerful and determined approach is needed. The crack is less help than it ought to be, although a combination of laybacking and using small fingerholds well left of the crack is what is needed. *In situ* protection is sound, with three pegs on this steepest section; shorties will find clipping the third peg a little gripping, as they will have to commit themselves to a layback position first, but good footholds and a big undercut wait above. From the good undercut, the bolt runner can be clipped and a tricky traverse left can be made to a narrow ledge, followed by an apelike swing and pull up to good holds. Now the climbing is all in balance, and the little groove up and right is soon sorted out to good undercuts below the last bulge. A few more steep pulls are needed before the easier angled top section leads past some detached-looking rock to the top.

Although not the hardest E4 6a around, Survival of the Fastest is an excellent test of determination and stamina, the generous *in situ* protection allowing E4 leaders to get on to territory with the sort of sustained level of difficulty normally reserved for E5.

All of these routes were the work of Stuart Cathcart, who seems to have had the place completely to himself up to the publication of his 1983 guidebook. It was inevitable then that some new faces would appear, and not surprising that the likes of Gary Gibson would soon become involved in the new-route scene here. Since 1983 there has been a steady stream of new routes, but not the rush that the nearby Ormes experienced. Perhaps that is why, with all too many people concentrating their efforts at Pen Trwyn, Cathcart's guide, with its unfashionable grading system, was passed by and ignored. Perhaps a certain amount of suspicion surrounding the author did not help, as his reputation had already been smudged in North Wales. Whatever the facts behind those stories, however, Cathcart's contribution to Clwyd climbing is outstanding and none of the subsequent pioneers has quite matched it in quantity.

Which is not to say that subsequent routes have lacked quality. Among the more recent additions are ones as fine as the best Peak District pitches. All along the escarpment there have been high-grade additions, with the unfortunately short walls at Pinfold North and

Dinbren North (the Alison Walls) seeing some particularly good routes from Gibson, John Moulding and John Codling. These latter two between them also took on the development of the Nemesis wall to the right of Survival of the Fastest. Apart from a characteristically bold foray from Pat Littlejohn, Friday the Thirteenth, which the two Johns subsequently straightened out and redescribed (in this case almost certainly improving on the original!), they have had the wall to themselves, producing the outstanding-looking routes of Manic Mechanic, Smoking Gun and Tres Hombres. It is difficult to pick any one of these above the others, but Manic Mechanic has a great deal of merit as a line, is full of surprises and is also marginally the easiest, at E5 6b. The wall overhangs gently for all of its 130 feet, and it is capped by bulges. Clearly all the routes are strenuous and sustained, and most utilize fixed protection to some degree, sometimes from previous aid routes.

Manic Mechanic was first climbed in 1984 by the two Johns, but using rests. It took an in-form Andy Pollitt to free the pitch completely a little later. The route initially used two bolt runners, both of which have long since gone, but there is still some sound fixed gear; wires are definitely needed though. The climbing is both strenuous and committing, with a very sustained first half and exciting positions on the second. The route begins just right of a whitebeam tree, some 25 feet right of Survival of the Fastest, below a groove leading up to a black ramp. This ramp seems to suffer from seepage all year, but unless it is very bad, it should still be climbable.

One friend recommended Manic Mechanic as better than either Supersonic or Bastille on High Tor, and having recently seconded Alan on Bastille, I had no hesitation in pointing him at this route and settling back to enjoy seconding! Looking up from the ground, it was hard to see any gear or holds near the base of the ramp, but after fiddling in a wire under the bulge to the right, soon he was reaching up for what had looked like a poor edge. I was a bit surprised when he seemed to relax completely on finding this edge, and started fiddling a good Rock 3 up and left.

'Is that any good, then?'

'Yeah, it's good – but it's chipped!'

Getting established on the ramp involved using a wet layaway, but the undercut above allowed for some time to wipe hands before reaching up right above the bulge.

'This one's chipped as well.'

A peg beckoned above, and a long reach found an improved hold next to it. A further undercut allowed a strenuous move to gain more chipped holds, and a long reach then found the next break and a further peg.

'You want to see this one, it's enormous.'

Sure enough, a large bucket chipped out at the break provides a good shake-out. Above is an obvious flake, and gaining it would probably have been tricky if it were not for …

'I don't believe this, the whole thing's on chipped holds!'

In the next break, a peg and jugs mark the end of the first 'pitch' and a good rest out left can allow you to shake your hands and your head.

'How does the top look?'

'It looks hard, but I'm sure there'll be something up there.'

A thread and some indifferent wires lead you to the roof, and a rest good enough to wonder how you get round that! A good peg up and left, about six inches above the bulge, is the key: gaining it is hard, but the hold you are going to use is right next to it. Summon all your strength and get as high as you can before stretching up to the incipient crack above: reach it with a straight arm and you will probably not be able to use it, so get high first. If you make it, the rest is a scramble.

It is impossible to see how such a major piece of chipping could have been contemplated, let alone achieved. The Manic Mechanic must have wielded large tools to wreak such damage: Manic Mutilation might be a more appropriate name. Isolated and rarely visited, it's not surprising that this has happened to Craig Arthur: there's nobody to complain or care. It's a pity that such an idyllic spot, and such a fine wall, has become such a crazy monument to the human ego. The BMC agreed policy of no chipping/improving of holds came too late for routes like this – and many others – and it is sad that the new guidebook makes no reference to these mistakes.

It would be wrong to be put off by this, though, as only an interest from outside the area will prevent further occurrences. If you haven't yet experienced the charms of the Eglwyseg Valley, then you now know what you've been missing. The fact that the whole escarpment is so unfrequented by climbers is part of its charm, so don't all go at once. And if any one section is busy, move along: with four miles to go at, it should be possible to find a bit of peace! Even if it doesn't attract people, Craig Arthur certainly catches the wind; pick the right day and you won't be disappointed.

Holy Island and Llandudno

■ *LOCATION* • Rhoscolyn, a short walk from the village of Rhoscolyn on the south-western side of Holy Island, Anglesey. Craig Pen Trwyn, above the privately owned 'Marine Drive' on the headland of the Great Orme, Llandudno. The Diamond, the central one of a number of cliffs on the Little Orme peninsula, Llandudno.

■ *ROUTES* • The Sun(E3 5c), Plumbline (E3 5c), Warpath (E5 6a), Wall of the Evening Light (A2/E6 6b)

■ *FIRST ASCENTS* • The Sun – Paul Williams, Jim Moran (1984); Plumbline – Rowland Edwards (1973); Warpath – Jim Moran, Paul Williams (1984); Wall of the Evening Light – Rowland Edwards (1972), first free ascent by Andy Pollitt (1988), with some variation in line.

■ *CONSIDERATIONS* • Rhoscolyn is part of an SSSI, and cars should be parked carefully on the ground in front of Rhoscolyn church. Craig Pen Trwyn has various restrictions, the essence of which is no climbing before 6 p.m. during the school summer holidays and over the Easter and Whit Bank Holiday weekends. In addition, certain routes are banned due to unstable rock, and the routes' position above the Marine Drive. The Diamond is subject to a bird ban from 1 March to 15 August.

■ *GUIDEBOOKS* • *Rock Climbing in Snowdonia* by Paul Williams (Constable, 1990); *Gogarth* by Andy Newton, Andy Pollitt, Steve Haston and Paul Williams (Climbers' Club, 1990); *North Wales Limestone RockFax* by Steve Mayers (Vertical Brain, 1992).

For an area so renowned for its mountains and mountain crags, it is perhaps unfair that Snowdonia is blessed with some remarkable sea-cliffs. Poor old Norfolk, miles from anything over three feet in height, didn't come out of the great rock distribution lottery very well in comparison. Within easy reach of Llanberis lie the wildly different environments of the Lleyn peninsula, with routes to rival some of the best north Cornish extravaganzas, featuring all sorts of interesting rock and protection; Anglesey, with its dramatic situations and committing masterpieces on fair rock and protection; and the Great Orme, characterized (a little unfairly) as being all tights and tantrums on excellent rock with mainly bolt protection.

In the past, the advantage of having all these areas so close by meant that it was nearly always possible to find something to do as a second best when the mountains were cloaked in their customary mists. The position at two of these venues is now almost the reverse, with many visitors to Pen Trwyn and Gogarth making these cliffs their prime objectives. Generally, all three areas enjoy better weather than the mountains, and with a careful eye on the wind direction, it really is often possible to find one or more of the sea-cliffs in good condition, even when it is pouring with rain at Llanberis.

The development of each area is an interesting history lesson in itself, and illustrates very well the effects of both fashion and attitudes to protection. It is fascinating to note that the 'adventure' new-route scene on Anglesey and the Lleyn peninsula is as healthy as ever, if not better than before, and it is certainly not suffering from the 'sport' climbing development of the Ormes. All three are very accessible to local and visiting climbers, and between them they have sufficient space to absorb and sustain both styles of climbing – a combination which has created a natural balance that suits most climbers. Indeed, the equipping of Pen Trwyn with belay bolts has been almost essential to maintain any access to the crags above the Marine Drive, so the general attitude to fixed protection here does not seem unreasonable.

The Lleyn peninsula is an amazing place to climb, very reminiscent of north Cornwall or north Pembroke. There are some big crags here too, with some really excellent lines on them. As half the fun here is exploration – there is no up-to-date guidebook – I shall not say anything else, but for anybody who relishes the prospect of feeling decidedly 'out there', alone, on a big route, with nobody around to get you out of difficulty, then this area is a must.

Gogarth has always been one of my favourite areas, and it certainly accounts for many of my most frightening climbing moments. It is really remarkable how the crag generates such a powerful atmosphere, especially since it is no longer totally isolated. For me it is definitely a place for the big routes, and I have found myself two or three times driving over just for the day to do one route. I never seem to have the mental energy – let alone physical energy – to do more than one of these big routes in a day, so there is sometimes the need to look around for a short pitch or two to finish the day off – and that was how I discovered Rhoscolyn.

On first sight, Rhoscolyn looks a friendly little place. A short and very pleasant stroll across fields leads to a coastguard lookout tower, from where the top of the first section of crag can be seen. They look so small these cliffs, especially if you've just come from the Main Cliff at Gogarth. What isn't obvious, though, is that much of the rock is very steep, and many of these short routes pack in a tremendous amount of climbing. There are three areas at Rhoscolyn, and all have worthwhile routes, but the first area, Llawder, holds the two real gems of the crag, the Sun and Warpath.

The Sun is the classic line at Rhoscolyn. A superb groove, perched above a large leaning flake at the foot of the wall, it is like one of those drawings inspired by Escher; you can never really work out what angle everything is set at because there is no real guide-line to work against. The main groove is both leaning rightwards (as you look at the cliff) and slightly overhanging, but as the groove is deep enough to accommodate a fair bit of bridging, it never really feels steep, in contrast to the merely vertical wall you traverse across to gain the groove-line. The route is best climbed in one pitch, then the second can enjoy watching the leader from a comfortable position. Gaining the base of the groove from the right is quite intimidating, although relatively straightforward, and it has defeated at least one party. The crux follows, with some determination needed to fight up the short steep wall until a bridging position can be reached at the base of the groove proper. From here, superb holds and runners lead up the corner, with a strenuous bit of jamming to pass the bulge in the right wall. Above here, easier, though now remarkably exposed climbing leads up and right to the top.

If the feeling on The Sun is definitely one of being on a bigger route, that feeling is exaggerated beyond all reasonable explanation on Warpath. The arête to the left of The Sun is only 125 feet long, yet it is cumulatively difficult, and works up a tremendous amount of exposure. The route begins way to the left of the arête on a poor grassy ledge, and the exposure starts straight away with a delicate rising traverse from the ledge out to a slabby area of rock, and a good rest. Already you have 50 feet of air beneath you, despite only gaining 15 feet of height from the belay. The slab above is not difficult, but it gradually steepens and narrows as the arête becomes more definitely formed. Above, a band of overhangs looks formidable, but excellent protection and bomb-proof jams carry you round the bulge on to the upper wall. The position is now sensational, and all of a sudden the holds disappear: only vertical, this wall forms the technical crux, with a number of 6a moves on small holds. There is additional protection to back up the peg runner, but it would be a strong and calm leader who has the time to place it. Soon, however, if all has gone well, a ledge is reached, and a few easier moves gain the top. A route of Gogarth stature, yet so accessible and short!

Rhoscolyn was developed in an incredibly short period in 1984, but it is only really a small crag. The previous summer it was not Anglesey that was in the headlines, but the limestone of Craig Pen Trwyn on the Great Orme. During that year, a whole colony of talented climbers descended on the crag with the intention of dragging it into line with other areas; and with a gradual acceptance of bolt protection, the crag has matured into a major forcing ground. There are now literally hundreds of excellent routes in this area, although some are currently banned due to an agreement with the local council regarding the stability of certain bits of rock and their proximity to the Marine Drive. It is impossible to pick even a selection of good routes from the many on offer, but it is certainly worth making it very clear that Pen Trwyn is not just for climbers who lead hard Extremes. There are now an increasing number of bolted easier routes on Lower Pen Trwyn, and some of the mid-grade Extremes on the main crag that are mainly nut-protected are excellent.

Plumbline, for example, is just that: probably the only really natural line on the cliff, a superb shallow chimney/groove that is now getting visibly polished. Driving along the Marine Drive for about half a mile, the line is quite obvious – just left of a large corner in the rock and about 100 yards before the road bends round to the left. Being able to park your car near by is only an advantage if you didn't have to pay to get in, so arrive early! This also ensures you get a little sunshine, as this side of the crag spends the afternoon in the shade. Despite the polish, it is a very classy route, full of technical interest for its 5c grade, and just sustained and steep enough to warrant the E3 grade. As an introduction to the area, it serves well in one respect, although the lack of bolts shows the route to belong to an earlier age. Fortunately, you can practise lowering off the big belay bolts though! It is sad that routes like this are now becoming ignored in favour of the rebolted Yellow Wall routes, for example, which really are not as good.

As you belay your partner from the quite worn base of the crag, and the sun slowly moves off the rock, look out across Llandudno bay and let your eyes wander over the Little Orme. Still visited much less than its neighbour, despite the addition of a number of modern bolted routes, the Little Orme has a brooding aspect, appearing almost to rise out of the sea like a whale. Towards the left-hand end, especially if the sun has started to glint over there – you will be able to pick out an enormous wall, rising the full height of the headland. This is Detritus Wall, home to one of the most amazing first ascents in British rock climbing, when Rowland Edwards soloed the 550-foot aid route, Detritus. Although much of the ground had already been climbed, daring to set out solo on to such a wall in 1970 was a major achievement. Detritus has been attacked by many fine climbers, but it is yet to go free, although it almost certainly will do so.

Further right, and almost in the centre of the mass of cliffs making up the Little Orme, lies the Diamond, a crag with immense scope for the future. Two years after Detritus, Edwards forced yet another huge route up this piece of rock in some 16 hours, calling it the Wall of the Evening Light. The first three pitches were aided, and then HVS-standard free climbing led to the top, the whole giving 500 feet of sensational climbing. In late 1986, inspired by a strange fit of exploritis, I managed to persuade two others to join me on a big adventure here, aiming to repeat the aid route in a slightly quicker time than the first ascent (it was November). Setting out at first light, we gingerly waded out to the boulder beach beneath the Diamond. This requires a fair degree of planning, as the lowest tide still ensures wet feet. Laden with spare clothing, six ropes, three full racks of slings, nuts and karabiners, an ice hammer and a claw hammer and about 20 pegs, we eventually gathered, wet feet and hot heads, at the foot of this wall. We had not come to look: we meant business.

What followed was one of the best day's climbing I have ever had, with a very real degree of fun combining with the cold and plenty of fear to produce quite delirious exhaustion. At one point, after a slow start, we decided we all had to climb together, 30 feet apart. This would probably have worked, but for the weight of the wet clothes and spare food in the rucksack attached to the last man (myself). Having set off at a rush, I had made quite a bit of ground on the second man, when a poor skyhook placement in a shallow scoop crumbled, under this extra weight of course. I ended up 20 feet lower, regretting the slack I had put into the system, and causing Tom some painful moments. I decided to haul the sack on a spare rope, and set off again, at a more leisurely pace suited to the others. While dawdling on a couple of sections, I began to think about the idea of free climbing this line. Although the angle and length seemed to suggest this was unlikely, the rock was, in fact, covered in holds. Apart from the odd bit of loose rock, the generally poor nature of the pegs and the difficulties in getting here in the first place, it appeared an obvious candidate to be freed. Well before we reached the top, at one o'clock in the morning, I was convinced that this would one day be transformed into a major, albeit very hard, free climb.

Some 20 months later – sooner than I would have thought – it was free climbed: a futuristic effort from Andy Pollitt, the true inheritor of Edwards's vision in this area. Although Pollitt bypassed the initial bulges, I was staggered that it was graded at E6 6b, much easier than I would have guessed, and equipped with fixed gear to go for. Admittedly, the problem of access was not immediately solved, but since then a rubber dinghy seems to have become the favourite method of access, allowing quite short visits to climb short routes to be made, with an easy return to the promenade.

In 1991, Steve Mayers tidied the job up by freeing the true start to Wall of the Evening Light, creating the superb-looking Specular Reflections. Out of the reach of most climbers, at a good E7, I can only testify that there really are holds there! I have yet to return to sample the delights of free climbing on this wall, but I am sure that these routes must be among the finest of their type anywhere in the world.

Bank Holiday Climbs

■ *LOCATION* • Pencoed pillar of Craig Cau, Cader Idris, high above the Idris Gates car park on the A487 Dolgellau to Machynlleth road. Clogwyn-yr-Eryr, tucked away at the head of the Crafnant valley, approached from Trefriw on the B5106 Betws-y-Coed to Conwy road. Craig-y-Clipiau, high above the slate tips that overlook the village of Tanygrisiau, in the Moelwyns.

■ *ROUTES* • Darker Angel (E3 5c), Astoroth/Snowdrop Connection (E3 6a), Clonus Left Hand (E3 6a), The Crimson Cruiser (E5 6a).

■ **FIRST ASCENTS** • Darker Angel – Dave Shaw, Keith Bentham (1974); Astoroth/Snowdrop Connection – Pete Gomersall, Pete Livesey (1978); Clonus Left Hand – Pete Livesey, Pete Gomersall (1980); the Crimson Cruiser – Ron Fawcett (1980).

■ **CONSIDERATIONS** • Darker Angel is best approached from above, necessitating a two-hour walk in, and it will only be climbable in a prolonged spell of good weather. For Clogwyn-yr-Eryr, cars can be parked at the head of the Crafnant Valley, just after the last gate: do not go further up the track to the hut itself.

■ **GUIDEBOOKS** • *Rock Climbing in Snowdonia* by Paul Williams (Constable, 1990) – this guide covers all the described routes; *Mid-Wales* by John Sumner (Climbers' Club, 1988) – for Darker Angel; *Tremadog and Cwm Silyn* by Mark Petty, Dave Farrant and Geoff Milburn (Climbers' Club, 1989) – for Crimson Cruiser.

THE NEXT time you wake up to perfect sunshine on a Bank Holiday Monday in North Wales, consider each of these three ways of spending the day as alternatives to queuing for a route on Cloggy or the Cromlech. I can't guarantee solitude, even though that has been my experience at each of these venues on three successive Bank Holidays, but I doubt if you will have to wait long.

Option one: Darker Angel on Cader Idris. Mid-Wales is a much better developed climbing area than many people know. It is yet another of those places to have suffered slightly from access problems and poor publicity, and the history of climbing in Mid-Wales revolves around very few people. It has heritage though, with the Great Gully on Craig Cau first being ascended by no less than Haskett Smith and O. G. Jones themselves, in 1895. I had spent a couple of tantalizing weekends exploring Craig Cywarch (in the rain) and the quarries around Barmouth, and my overall impressions of Mid-Wales were not good. Then a new guidebook arrived, and with the rush of enthusiasm that any such occasion seems to bring, I snapped up a copy and eagerly planned my next ten weekends. However, the rain kept falling, and the guidebook joined the ones to Squamish (I never made it to Ireland, let alone Canada) and Skye (total time spent on Skye before buying guidebook – eight weeks; total time spent on Skye after buying guidebook – none!). As it happened, the next visit I made to North Wales was on a Bank Holiday weekend, and although the idea of visiting Mid-Wales had not been well received by my companions, I sneaked the guidebook in my rucksack anyway, determined to make a bit of an effort to get them there on the Monday.

By Sunday night the omens were looking good. We had climbed on

Gogarth, on Slate and on the Cromlech, and I sensed weariness and mellowness in the team. I waited until about eleven, when the glazed look had appeared in their eyes, and then pulled out the guide from under the table, flashing the stunning cover photograph round the table: 'What about that, then?' We had already agreed that a bit of exploring was a suitable activity for the morrow, and I knew no one wanted to push themselves too hard.

'It looks brilliant; where is it?' The route was Darker Angel, and the crag was Craig Cau, on Cader Idris. 'Hang on, I've walked up there – it's miles!' I had to agree that the approach looked impressive, but I sensed success.

'Three-quarters of an hour, so I'm told.' Fortunately nobody was alert enough to check who had told me, and the plan was in the bag. 'We can finish early and get home before the rush.' I read the description again: 'destined to become one of the great Welsh classics,' just in case.

Monday was as fine a day as you could ask for; for some reason my childhood memories of North Wales at holiday times always involve rain, but my recent experience contradicts that. We packed up and headed south, to the Idris Gates car-park. Before long we were tramping up through the woods, sweating already in the heat of the morning air. Of course, it took an hour just to get to the beautiful Llyn Cau, at which point we could assess the crag.

'It looks a bit chossy,' murmured the most reluctant member of the party. I wouldn't have dared to agree, but I had already thought the same. The lower pitches of Darker Angel follow a VDiff for some distance, before breaking out right and round into the Great Gully, which we couldn't see from the lake. All the same it didn't look much fun.

'It's the top two pitches we've come to do,' I suggested, 'so why don't we walk round to the top and abseil in?' Mutiny quelled, smiles returned and once again we were off. The other two headed off towards the infamous sounding Crack of Cau, supposedly HVS, but you could just tell that it would be harder!

Eventually, two hours (including a very brief swim) after setting out, we stood on the top of Darker Angel, and we could see why it would be a classic: the positions looked superb, high up on this steep gully wall, even though there was no sun on the rock. Carefully, we rigged an abseil that would allow us to pull the ropes and geared up. Suffice it to say that a single abseil just gains the stance beneath the first 5c pitch (pitch 4), but that the abseil rope should be knotted at the end: it's a long way down. A bit of swinging around is needed to get on to the stance, but more worrying than that was what we had seen on the way down: green rock; not greenstone but green in coating – a thick, wet, lichenous coating as if a tin of paint had been poured down the rock. We had a moment's debate as to whether we should pull the ropes, then committed ourselves, praying that they did not snag. The care taken in setting up the abseil paid off, and we plunged from the sunny, close-cropped grass top to a tiny ledge in the middle of a huge, dank, sunless wall!

Before you wonder why this merits a description at all, let me say that the climbing is brilliant, and were the route to be clean, and approached in this fashion from above, I have no doubt that it would be a superb classic. The rock is solid, the protection adequate, the moves technical and the positions are exciting. The tricky slab that starts pitch two was wet, but it was still climbable without much change in the grade. We felt like pioneers from the 1950s! Looking down from that first belay – and talking to people who have done the VDiff in its entirety – I seriously doubt the worth of the approach from below. Perhaps there are years when a couple of early ascents clean the winter's growth, and the climb remains in condition for the rest of the summer, but I am fairly sure that our end of August visit was the first that year. For all that, it was enjoyable, and we have had many good laughs about the other team failing to reach the foot of the Crack of Cau!

However, every time I have tried to persuade the team to revisit Mid-Wales, I have had no joy, and their feeling is definitely one of a superb experience, unexpected and never to be repeated. For myself, I still plan weekends there, but the rain always returns to thwart my plans: perhaps those childhood memories were right after all.

Option two: Clogwyn-yr-Eryr. I had talked about going to the Crafnant Valley almost every weekend I had been in North Wales since 1981, when I first read about the supposedly excellent routes that had been done there. Something better always came up though, and it wasn't until 1989 that I eventually made it there. Driving up the Crafnant Valley is a pleasure in itself, the combination of the narrow road and picturesque scenery making you feel more in the Lake District than in Snowdonia. Once at the end of the road, Clogwyn-yr-Eryr is unmissable: the groove-seamed cliff standing at the head of the valley. Parking is possible just inside the last gate, and a path leads off to the right, through woods and then back up left to the scree beneath the crag. On closer acquaintance, you soon realize how steep the rock is, with a number of severely undercut starts to the imposing groove-lines. All the routes are good, but the two lines that dominate the main arête of the buttress, Clonus Left Hand and Phoenix, and the obvious V-groove and head-wall of Astoroth/Snowdrop are excellent, and all good-value E3 6a. The rock is traditional mountain rhyolite, and not always solid on the first two routes, although immaculate on the last one.

Clonus Left Hand starts just right of the main arête, beneath some daunting bulges that guard the leftmost groove on the front of the buttress. It is not a good route to warm up on, the start being both bold and very sustained. The bulge is taken on good holds, but without protection until a good thread in a jug at 25 feet. This commitment is then matched by a very technical sequence up the groove, fortunately with good protection, until a few moves left bring the arête and an easing of angle. It is possible to belay here, but better to keep going and enjoy the relatively straightforward, but marvellously positioned, top arête. It is one of those routes where the easier upper section is far from being an anti-climax to what has gone before; indeed, it extends the pleasure by warming down those over-exerted muscles and easing the mind back to normal. An abseil descent is possible from some fixed slings (giving you a free look at Phoenix).

The intriguing groove of Astoroth is a different sort of proposition. Very safe, but seemingly holdless! I ended up almost facing outwards, with a definite chimneying movement needed to gain height where the groove is blankest. The transition back to facing in to pull on the superb jugs thus reached is awkward, and the sudden feeling of exposure makes this a thrilling pitch in its own right. However, it is just the hors d'oeuvre for the top pitch of Snowdrop, the stunning crack-line in the gently leaning wall up and left. This provides a brilliant series of moves, with excellent (although strenuous to place) protection. The finger jams and holds on the wall are all good, but the angle makes it a bit of a fight!

On reflection, I don't regret not visiting the Crafnant Valley earlier, as the routes are still as brilliant as they were when first done. Finding the crag empty on a Bank Holiday suggests that it will be possible to enjoy such superb climbing in beautiful surroundings, without the need to queue, for a long while to come.

Option three: Crimson Cruiser. The advantage of somewhere like Craig-y-Clipiau on a Bank Holiday is obvious. As there is really only one route there that most extreme climbers are likely to want to do, very few people will make the effort to go there on a day when they will want to get lots of climbing done. This isn't the right attitude though, as the quality of the one pitch is such that the lack of quantity should be easily forgiven by the discerning climber, and walking round the slate tips can provide more than enough interest and exercise for the rest of the day. If necessary, there are other good pitches in the area, including Non Dairy Creamer, the wall to the right of Crimson Cruiser, although the direct start to this is both harder and more serious than the guidebook suggests.

Craig-y-Clipiau is an undistinguished little crag. Tucked away among the ruined buildings and slate tips above the village of Tanygrisiau, it is a crag that is remarkably lacking in stars. There are other crags in the Moelwyns that provide consistently better routes in nicer surroundings, but there is no doubt that Crimson Cruiser is the single best route hereabouts. A hanging prow is the substance of the route, and the reason it is so good is partly due to the climbing being so much easier than it looks. The pitch as a whole overhangs some 20 feet in 130 feet, yet there is an abundance of reasonable holds – at their best towards the top when the angle is steepest. The E5 grade is merited though, as there are some bold moves, and the position towards the top can combine, with some of the holds being hidden, to cause some tense moments.

The route starts up the innocuous-looking slab beneath the traverse of Mean Feet, a good HVS. This is harder than it looks, and bold in places, but the traverse line is soon reached, and good runners placed. An awkward move up right on to a ledge follows, and then the substance of the route begins. Stepping left into the groove is tricky, but climbing it is even harder, with some intricate moves up to a small ledge and a semi-rest. The protection is fair, but this section is strenuous and the arms start to tire. Now commit yourself to the wall above and, using good pockets, pull up to gain a larger ledge and another rest. Above, the prow leans dramatically, so place all the gear you can, psyche up and then go, aiming for the very crest of the prow, where superb jugs quickly lead to the top.

You must be very serious about climbing if you really need to do something else after that. The Moelwyns are a good area for the middle- to lower-grade climber; let the relaxed atmosphere of the place rub off a little on to you, and enjoy the rest of the Bank Holiday lazing in the sun.

Dinorwic Slate

- ■ *LOCATION* • The Dinorwic slate quarries, on the other side of the Llyn Padarn and Llyn Peris lakes from Llanberis. Pull My Daisy and Ride the Wild Surf are on the Rainbow Slab and Colossus Wall, best approached from Padarn Country Park. Central Sadness is in California, reached from the bus turning circle at Dinorwic.

- ■ *ROUTES* • Pull My Daisy (E2 5c), Ride the Wild Surf (E4 6a), Central Sadness (E5 6a).

- ■ *FIRST ASCENTS* • Pull My Daisy – Mark Lynden (1984); Ride the Wild Surf – Paul Williams (1986); Central Sadness – John Silvester, Chris Dale (1986).

- ■ *CONSIDERATIONS* • On these routes the slate is of superb quality. The slate quarries are often dry when the main Llanberis Pass cliffs are damp, drying almost instantly after rain. In rain, though, they become particularly slippery.

- ■ *GUIDEBOOK* • *Llanberis* by Paul Williams (Climbers' Club, 1987).

THE VAST mass of quarries created by the building of the Dinorwic power station are undoubtedly a visual blot on the North Wales landscape. However, they are now host to some very fine routes which have increased the options for local and visiting climbers alike. The sheer numbers of climbers operating in the Llanberis Pass on sunny weekends suggests that the environmental loss from the creation of the quarries may be compensated for slightly by the reduced wear and tear on the scree leading up to the mountain crags! It is certainly true that climbing in North Wales is now a threat to the environment, and if the people who regularly troop to the slate quarries would otherwise have been adding to the congestion on Dinas Mot, then the artificial playground the CEGB have created should not, perhaps, be viewed too critically. As the quarries seem to be increasingly incorporated into Padarn Country Park, then climbers with an environmental conscience should view them sympathetically, rather than as a sad loss – wildlife seems to thrive there.

From a purely climbing point of view, the quarries are certainly a gain. Climbing on slate is always interesting, and the diversity of the quarries – in size, angle of rock and solidity – makes for a variety of experiences. Add to this the peculiar historical quirk that the bulk of the routes were first done in the mid-1980s – when bolts were becoming accepted by some climbers but still denounced by others – and you have all tastes of route from the ultimate sports climb (bolts and manufactured holds) right through to the very bold (on-sight solo on creaky holds). The rock does not lend itself to easier climbs, the fracturing process in slate creating lots of smooth slabs and sheer walls, with few crack-lines: when cracks do occur they are often in smooth faces and offer few footholds outside the crack.

In the Extreme grade, however, there are many classics; indeed, on the Rainbow Slab virtually every route is a classic! This superb piece of rock, 150 feet high and over 200 feet wide, is the essential slate slab, hosting products of both the extremely bold and extremely safe variety, with examples of both to a high technical standard. There are few natural features on the slab, the most obvious being a vertical pillar of rock stuck on at the top, just left of centre, and a curious ripple that runs up and then across the slab, like a rainbow. Just left of its start, the naturally protected but very difficult crack-line of Naked Before the Beast runs up the full height of the crag. All the routes to the right of it are excellent, though all are difficult and require a good head as well as great finger strength: the ripple itself forming the substance of one of the best routes on slate, the Rainbow of Recalcitrance, a very bold E6 that requires a high degree of competence from the second as well as the leader. The climbing on the Rainbow can be sampled at a more reasonable grade just to the left of Naked Before the Beast, where a more pronounced crack-line runs up to a short metal spike. This is Pull My Daisy, a superb pitch. The start is a little off-putting, but a good indication of what is to follow: a few quick pulls on small but positive ledges without protection. Once the crack proper is gained, progress is normally brisk to the spike. This can be tied off and the section above surveyed. The crack ends, but above, a shallow ramp runs up leftwards. The crux is getting established on the ramp, some of the holds being unobvious, but then the fun begins. There is no further protection and, although the route is graded E2 5c, it feels more like an E2 5b up here, then an E2 5a, maintaining excitement right to the top; never quite becoming easy enough to switch off your concentration, but never really being hard enough to warrant a rescue; and after all, it is a slab, so you can take all the time in the world. Pull My Daisy is an excellent introduction to slate climbing, and gives you a real taste of the slate slab experience.

Slate is not just about slabs; just round to the left of the Rainbow Slab, and impressive enough were it not for its neighbour, is the steep Colossus Wall. Although the obvious line, Colossus E3, often seeps, the majority of the wall is immaculate clean slate – 150 feet of strength-sapping vertical rock, covered in basically good holds. Unlike the Rainbow Slab, where stars are thrown about like confetti, there is only one truly classic line up this wall, but it is magnificent. Ride the Wild Surf takes a shallow leftwards-facing corner line just left of the centre of the face, and it is as good an E4 6a as you can get. Well bolted, the route is very safe, but there is still potential for some large falls if the fingers uncurl high up!

The start is as obvious as it is difficult: a small hanging groove lies just left of a huge, crudely chipped hold. Climb up to the chipped hold, pull up rightwards and then stand in it. The problem is to get established in the groove; there is no easy way, and a combination of laybacking the edge of the groove and smearing the left foot out on the left wall, perhaps with a wild lunge for the ledge above, seems to do the trick. I have done the route three times now, and each time found a slightly different sequence, though I have never found it any easier! Once established, the next 50 feet are great fun. Big holds lead up the corner without any real difficulty, past a handful of bolts, to a small roof. A small run out livens up proceedings here, but again the holds are good, and the degree of excitement will depend on how tired you have started to feel. Once at the next bolt, however, you are faced with the second crux, an 'enigmatic' groove: I have always found it best to bridge the next section, which although precarious involves less pain in the fingers, but it is possible to pull hard instead. Either way a good ledge is quickly reached, and a decisive bit of mantling is the best way to get on to it. From here the difficulties ease, though by now most people's arms will be feeling the strain, and by the time you have reached the top you will know you have climbed a full rope length!

The Rainbow area tends to attract a good number of people, partly because the slab is so impressive to look at and partly because of the bolts on the Colossus Wall. Many visitors spend more time looking than climbing, and you can start to feel a little 'on show'. Other parts of the quarries are even busier, with Bus Stop quarry (obvious from the bus turning circle) probably the most popular. Both of these areas are easily accessible, with Bus Stop being a particularly good bet for a quick visit. There are a number of less accessible quarries, some which have an almost mountain-like atmosphere.

One of the most interesting routes in the quarries can be found in one such area, California. I was drawn to this part of the quarries by the description of Central Sadness in Paul Williams's mould-breaking Llanberis guidebook. Apart from being described as 'tremendous' and 'great', it was the clever way in which the two pitches had been allocated as 'a pitch for heroes' and 'a pitch for the married man with a large rack of wires' that intrigued me. At various times in my climbing career I had seen myself as both of these, but, feeling very much the latter at the time, I had recruited a younger, fitter and sharper hero to sort out the first pitch, while I carried my treasury of battered wires for the second pitch. I ought to admit at this point that, being one of the élite club who has placed more than 25 runners in Comes the Dervish, slate cracks held no terrors for me! So, slightly apprehensive through a lack of any first-hand evidence, we set off for California.

Just the approach to it is fascinating, with a definite 'discovering a lost world' feel to it. From the bus-turning circle, a footpath runs into the quarries. This is followed until the obvious Dali's Hole on the left: obvious because it consists of a deep pool with trees growing out from the water like a surrealist painting (although the trees can be fully submerged at times, making it less obvious). Facing the pool, a small tunnel mouth can be seen atop a bank of scree up to the right. Work up to this tunnel, and, avoiding the inevitable puddles, go through it. On the far side you emerge in a giant vertical bore-hole, from which another tunnel leads into California itself, past some dramatic rock scenery.

Once in the quarry, you cannot fail to be struck by two things: the immense sweep of the California Wall, a smooth steep face broken only by a large ledge system beneath a cave on the left-hand side, and the vast stretch of unclimbed rock that forms the rest of the quarry! Admittedly, there are few obvious weaknesses, but the potential is surely there. Central Sadness takes the smooth wall at its highest point, the second pitch finishing up the obvious crack. It is a long route, over 200 feet, with two 6a pitches. The first is bold enough, but it is only actually hard at the start. This can be safely bouldered out if needs be, but my hero was up to the job and moved swiftly on to the meat of the pitch, a delicate 5b/c wall on large sloping holds and undercuts, fortunately less than vertical in angle. There are some runners, including a tape round a protruding block, but falling off is to be avoided. It is certainly an exhilarating pitch though, and the excellent stance equipped with two bolts (the only fixed gear) resulted in my hero stripping down to sunbathing gear, perhaps in anticipation of a long sojourn!

By the time I reached the belay, I was slightly apprehensive about the top pitch, as the E5 grade had yet to be earned! This, combined with the extremely generous lashing of bomb-proof wires I felt duty-bound to sink in the finger crack above, meant that my hero's expectations of a long rest were fulfilled, and, amazing even myself with my ability to stay in such a steep crack without falling off for so long, I duly fought my way to the top. This second pitch is a superb piece of climbing, with difficulties cumulating as you get higher, and the crux about 80 feet up, where the gradually increasing angle finally reaches vertical. A medley of technical little moves, laybacking the crack to get feet as high as possible, leads to a small bulge, and the only committing move on the pitch, a pull up rightwards to a reassuringly deep hand crack.

Completely different in character from both the bold Rainbow and Vivian slabs and the well-bolted Colossus Wall, it is hard to say that Central Sadness is the best route I have done on slate. I think it is certainly the most atmospheric though, and despite the excellent protection on pitch two it has a 'big' feel to it. It is almost inevitable that most of the enormous number of new routes yet to be done in the quarries will be bolted in their entirety, as the current trend seems to be to sacrifice quarried rock to the idol of sport climbing. Ride the Wild Surf shows how good bolted routes can be, and I think that the slate quarries of Dinorwic do accommodate such climbs, in such a man-made setting, perfectly well. It is interesting that even the practice of chipping holds, universally frowned upon, is almost celebrated here, among the ruined winding houses and rusty oil drums that seem to be held together by great lengths of cable that appear out of the ground and then disappear equally inexplicably. In this monument to man's ability to interfere with nature, it is good to have a legacy of fine unbolted routes like Pull My Daisy and Central Sadness so that future generations can judge our actions for themselves.

INDEX

Above and Beyond 69, 70
access restrictions
  Castlemartin Artillery Range 10
  Chapel Head Scar 93, 95
  Cheddar Gorge 30, 31
  The Diamond 109
  Great Overhanging Wall (GO Wall) 19
  Hoghton Quarry 98
  with Ministry of Defence 11–12
  Pen Trwyn 109
  Sandy Crag 85
  Swordfish 10
  Yellow Wall 6
Acid Rock 32–3
Ahimsa (E3 5c) 30, 32–3
Allen, John 67, 76
All Roads Lead to Rome (E5 6b) 98, 99, 102
Alsford, Emma 10
Amanita Muscarina (E4) 27
Amnesty (E2 5b) 45, 48
Android (E4 5c) 95–6
Andromeda Strain (E4/5) 48
Angel Fingers (E1 5b) 85, 87, 88
Anglesey 108, 109
Anstey's Cove 49, 53
Aplomb 73
Arms Race (E4 5c) 25, 28
Armstrong, Dave 89
Astoroth (E3 6a) 113, 116, 117
Aviation (E1 5b) 49, 50–1
Avon Gorge 25–9
  Amanita Muscarina (E4) 27
  Arms Race (E4 5c) 25, 28
  Clean Hand Gang 28
  Edgemaster (E5 6b) 25, 28–9
  Exploding Galaxy Wall 26–7
  Limbo (HVS 5b) 25, 26
  Main Wall 28
  Malbogies 28
  Piton Route 28
  Sea Walls 25, 28
  Suspension Bridge Buttress 25, 26
  Tour de France (E5/6) 27
  Upper Wall 25, 28
  Yellow Edge (E3 5b/c) 25, 27, 28

Badcock, P. 49
Baggy Point 36
Balcombe's Piton Route 28
Bancroft, Steve 67, 76
Ban-y-Gor 20
Baptist (E2 5c) 47
Barley, Robin 80
Barmouth quarries 114
Bartlett, S. 54
Bassett, D. 49
Bass Point 45, 49
  Amnesty (E2 5b) 45, 48
  Cull (E3 5b) 45, 48, 49
Bastille 107–8
Beachy Head x, 62–6
  Monster Crack (XS 5c) 62, 63–6
Bell, S. 45
Bennett, Fred 19
Bentham, Keith 114
Berlin (E5 6b) 15, 18–19
Berzins, Martin 82, 83
Bigger Splash (E3 5b) 3, 5
Bird of Paradise (E6) 34
Bishop, S. 45
Blasphemy (E2 5c) 76, 79
BMC see British Mountaineering Council
bolts ix, 42, 44, 74, 119
  ethical dilemmas 82–3
Bonington, Chris 28
Borrowdale
  Goat Crag 89
  Penal Servitude (E5 6b) 89, 91–2
  Rack 91

Reecastle Crag 89, 90–3
  Shepherd's Crag 89
  Watendlath 90–1
  White Noise (E3 5c) 89, 91
Bosherston Head 10, 14
British Mountaineering Council
  guidebooks 54
  policy on holds 108
Brown, Joe 67, 68, 69, 76, 78
Brown, R. 72
Buccaneer (E2 5b) 54, 56–7
Buckley, N. 54
Bude 36, 37
  Compass Point 39
Bull, P. 49
Buoux (France) 90
Burbage Valley 67–71
  Above and Beyond 69, 70
  Goliath (E5 6a) 67, 69–70
  Higgar Tor 68
  Long Tall Sally (E1 5b) 67, 68
  Offspring (E5 6b) 67, 70–1
  Rasp (E2 5b) 67, 68–9
  Silent Spring (E4 5c) 67, 70
  Wall Street Crash (E6 6c) 71
Burke, P. 59
Burning Giraffe (HVS) 22, 24

Cader Idris 113, 114–16
  Crack of Cau (HVS) 115–16
  Craig Cau 114, 115
  Darker Angel (E3 5c) 113, 114,
    115–16
  Great Gully 114, 115
Call to Arms (E4 5c) 49, 52–3
Cannings, F.E.R. 40, 41, 43, 49
Can't Buy a Thrill (E5 6b) 7
Carn Gowla 45–8
  America 46
  Andromeda Strain (E4/5) 48
  Awakening 47
  Baptist (E2 5c) 47
  Crystal Voyage 47
  Haze 47
  Mercury Connection (HVS) 47
  Mercury (E2 5b) 45–6, 46–7
Carn Kenidjack 46, 48
Carroll, Damian 10
Castlemartin Artillery Range 10, 13
Cathcart, Stuart 103, 106
Cave Route (Right Hand) (E6 6a) 80, 84
Central Sadness (E5 6a) 118, 121–2
Chambers, M. 30
Chapel Head Scar 93, 95–7

access restrictions 93, 95
  Android (E4 5c) 95–6
  For When The Tree Goes 95
  Great Buttress 95, 97
  Great Gully 97
  Lunatic (E4 5c) 93, 97
  Moonchild (E4 5c) 93, 96–7
  Phantom Zone 97
  Wargames 97
Cheddar Gorge 30–5
  access restrictions 30, 31
  Acid Rock 32–3
  Ahimsa (E3 5c) 30, 32–3
  Amphitheatre 31
  Bird of Paradise (E6) 34
  Coronation Street 32, 33, 35
  Crow (E3 5c) 30, 33, 34–5
  High Rock 32, 33
  loose rocks 31–2
  Paradise Lost (E5 6b) 30, 34
  Shoot Gully 34
  Spacehunter 34
  Sunset Buttress 32, 33–4
  West Route 33
  Zawn 31
Chee Dale 72–6
  Aplomb 73
  Clarion Call (E5 6a) 72, 74, 75
  Cosmopolitan (E6) 75
  Golden Mile (E5 6b) 75, 76
  Mad Dogs and Englishmen (E3 5c)
    72, 74
  Mortlock's Arête (E4) 75–6
  Sirplum (E1 5b) 72, 73
  Sloe Gin 73
Chepstow 19
Chew Valley 76
Citizen's Edge (E1 5c) 59, 60–1
Clarion Call (E5 6a) 72, 75
Clarke, Alan 67
Cleasby, Ed 93
Clogwyn du'ur Arddu x
Clogwyn-yr-Eryr 113, 116–17
  Astoroth (E3 6a) 113, 116, 117
  Clonus Left Hand (E3 6a) 113,
    116–17
  Phoenix 116, 117
  Snowdrop Connection (E3 6a) 113,
    116, 117
Clonus Left Hand (E3 6a) 113, 116–17
Clovelly 36, 41
Clwyd 103–8
  Craig Arthur 103, 104, 108
  Craig-y-Forwen 90, 104

Digitron (E2 5b) 103, 104–5, 106
Dinbren North (Alison Walls) 107
Eglwyseg Valley 103, 104, 108
Friday the Thirteenth 107
grading 105–6
Le Chacal (E2 5c) 104
Llangollen 103, 104
Manic Mechanic (E5 6b) 103, 107, 108
Manikins of Horror (E3 5c) 103, 105, 106
Nemesis wall 106, 107
Offa's Dyke footpath 103, 104
Ormes 106 *see also* Great Orme; Little Orme
Pinfold North 106
Smoking Gun 107
Survival of the Fastest (E4 6a) 103, 106, 107
Touch of Class (E2 5b) 104
Tres Hombres 107
World's End ford 103, 104
Coastguards 63
Codling, John 103, 107
Compass Point 39
Conger (E1 5c) 54, 57–8
Cornice 74, 75
Cornish, H. 49
Cornwall
Carn Gowla and Bass Point 45–9
Tintagel viii
Coronation Street 32, 33, 35
Cosmopolitan (E6) 75
Crack of Cau (HVS) 115–16
Cracked Actor (E2 5b) 98, 99, 100
Crafnant Valley 113, 116, 117
Craig Arthur 103, 104, 108
Craig Cau 114, 115
Craig Cywarch 114
Craig Pen Trwyn 106, 108, 109, 110, 111
Craig-y-Clipiau 113, 117–18
Crimson Cruiser (E5 6a) 113, 117–18
Non Dairy Creamer 117
Craig-y-Forwen 90, 104
Crewe, Richard 54
Crimson Cruiser (E5 6a) 113, 117–18
Crocker, Martin
in Southern England 62
in Wales 6, 7, 15
in West Country 25, 28, 30, 34
Crow (E3 5c) 30, 33, 34–5
Crowley, Aleister 63

Cull (E3 5b) 45, 48, 49
Culm coast 36, 37, 39–40
Blackchurch 39
Bude 36, 37, 39
Exmansworthy 39
Henna Cliff 39
Sacre Coeur (E2 5c) 39
Screda Point 39
Speke's Mill Mouth 39
Verger (E2 5a) 39
see also Lower Sharpnose Point
Curran, J. 59
Cwmaman Main Quarry 15, 16–17
Arête Buttress 16
Mother of Pearl (E4 6b) 15, 17

Dale, Chris 118
Darbyshire, Keith 36
Darker Angel (E3 5c) 113, 114, 115–16
Dartmoor x, 49–51
Aviation (E1 5b) 49, 50–1
Haytor 50
Interrogation (E3 6a) 49, 50
Low Man 50
Dawes, Johnny 67, 70
Dearman, Bob 72
Devon
Dartmoor x, 49–51
Lower Sharpnose Point 36–40
Torquay 51–3
Diamond, The 108, 112–13
Digitron (E2 5b) 103, 104–5, 106
Dinas Rock 15, 17–19
Berlin (E5 6b) 15, 18–19
Big Time 18
Giant Killer 17–18
Groovy Tube Day 17, 18
Kennelgarth Wall 17
Main Overhang 17, 18
Spain (E4 6a) 15, 18
Springboard 17
Dinbren North (Alison Walls) 107
Dinorwic slate quarries 118–22
Bus Stop 120
California 121
Central Sadness (E5 6a) 118, 121–2
Colossus Wall 120, 122
Comes the Dervish 121
Dali's Hole 121
Naked Before Beast 119
Pull My Daisy (E2 5c) 118, 119–20, 122
Rainbow of Recalcitrance (E6) 119
Rainbow Slab 119, 120, 122

Ride the Wild Surf (E4 6a) 118, 120, 122
Vivian slab 122
Divine Guiding Light (E7 6b) 7
Dixon, Nick 72, 75
Donnithorne, Paul 10
Doorpost, Lockwood's Chimney v
Doubting Thomas (E5 6b) 98, 100
Drake, Duncan 82
Drummond, Ed 25
Durlston Country Park 54

Earl, John 85, 86
Edgemaster (E5 6b) 25, 28–9
Edwards, Rowland 45, 109, 112
Eglwyseg Valley 103, 104, 108
Embankment (Chee Dale) 73
Empire of the Sun (E6 6b) 49, 53
Evans, Al 72
Exorcist (E3 5b) 40, 42–3, 44
Exploding Galaxy Wall 26–7
Exposure Explosion (HVS 5a) 1, 2

Fall Bay 5, 6–7
Farrell, R. 54
Fatti, Paul 40, 42, 43, 44
Fawcett, Ron 80, 84, 93, 96, 114
Fay (E4/5 6a) 36, 38
For When The Tree Goes 95
Fowler, Mick 49, 63
Frankie Comes Too Soon (E5 6b) 80, 82, 83
Freddie's Finale (HVS 5b) 76, 78
Friday the Thirteenth 107

Gibson, Gary
    in Devon and Cornwall 40, 43–4
    in Lancashire 99, 102
    in Peak District 72, 74, 75
    in Southern England 62
    in Wales 15, 19, 106, 107
Gloag, Terry 25
Glyn Neath 15
Goat Crag 89
Godding, John 49
Golden Mile (E5 6b) 75, 76
Goliath (E5 6a) 67, 69–70
Gomersall, Pete 83, 114
Gordale Scar 84
Gower 5–10
    Boiler Slab 6
    Can't Buy a Thrill (E5 6b) 7
    Divine Guiding Light (E7 6b) 7
    Dulfer 6

Fall Bay 5, 6–7
Fall Bay Buttress 7
Giant's Cave 7
Great Boulder Cove 5
Jesus Wept (E6 6a) 7
Mewslade Bay 5
Pat Littlejohn's Masterpiece (E6 6b) 7
Rhossili 5, 7
Thriller (E4 6a) 7
Thurba Head 6–7
Transformer (E3 5c) 6, 8, 9
Yellow Regeneration (E5 6b) 6, 8, 9
Yellow Wall (E3 5c) 5, 6, 7–9, 10
Gray, Dennis 80
Great Orme 106, 108, 109, 110, 111
Great Overhanging Wall (GO Wall) 21–4
Greenford Road (E5 6b) 85, 87, 88
gritstone climbing 68–71, 79
Grosnez Point 58, 59, 60
guidebooks vii, viii
    Avon and Cheddar 25, 30, 32, 34
    Borrowdale 89
    British Mountaineering Council's Routes series 54
    Chee Dale 72
    Clwyd Limestone 103
    Clwyd Rock 103
    Froggatt 67
    Gogarth 109
    Gower and South East Wales 1, 6, 15
    Jersey and Guernsey 59
    Jersey Rock 59
    Llanberis 118
    Mid Wales 114
    Moorland Gritstone: Chew Valley 77
    North Devon and Cornwall 36, 45, 49
    Northumberland Climbing Guide 85
    North Wales Limestone RockFax 109
    Peak Limestone 72
    Pembrokeshire 10
    Rock Climbing in Snowdonia 109, 114
    Rock climbs Lancashire and the North West 93, 98
    Scafell, Dow and Eskdale 93
    South Devon and Dartmoor 49
    Southern Sandstone 63
    South West Climbs 25, 36, 40, 45, 49, 54, 59
    Swanage 54
    Tremadog and Cwm Silyn 114
    Wye Valley 19
    Yorkshire Limestone 80, 81

Yorkshire Limestone RockFax 80
Yorkshire Limestone Supplement 83
Gurnard's Head 46

Hall, Brian 80
Harrison, R. 30, 54
Hart, Ed 49
Harwood, John 1
Haszko, R. 59
Heard, Charlie 10
Henna Cliff 39
Hepple 87
Higgar Tor 68
High Tor (Chee Dale) 72
Hill, W. 25
Hodge Close Quarry 94–5
  Ten Years After (E4 5c) 93, 94–5
Hoghton Quarry 98, 99, 100–2
Holy Island 108, 110–11
  Llawder 110
  Rhoscolyn 108, 110, 111
  The Sun (E3 5c) 109, 110–11
  Warpath (E5 6a) 109, 110
Horsfield, Clive 1
Houghton, A. 6
Hutchinson, Bob 85

Ichabod 93
insurance, third-party liability 31–2
Interrogation (E3 6a) 49, 50

jamming 50, 56
Jenkin, Gordon 54
Jersey 58–62
  Citizen's Edge (E1 5c) 59, 60–1
  Grosnez Point 58, 59, 60
  La Cotte de Sainte Brelade 59–60
  Le Pinacle 61, 62
  Les Landes 59, 60
  Le Vyi 61
  Open Heart Surgery (HVS 5a) 60
  Perihelion (HVS 5a) 59, 60
  Perry Coma (E5/6) 60
  Ragged Edge (E5) 60
  Rouge Nez 60
  Sorel Point 59
  Tax Exile (E5 6a) 59, 61
  Tête D'Ane 60
  Total Lack of Control (E2) 61
Jesus Wept (E6 6a) 7
Johnson, P. 25
Jones, O.G. 114
Jones, S. 45
jumping-off 86–7

Kangaroo Wall (E2 6a) 19, 22, 23
Kilnsey Crag 80, 82–3
King, Chris 6, 10, 19
Knighton, Dave 93

Ladram Bay 50
Lake District 89–97
  Borrowdale 89–93
  Southern Lakes 93–7
Lamb, Jeff 89
Lancashire 98–102
  Aladdinsane 99
  All Roads Lead to Rome (E5 6b) 98,
    99, 102
  Angelzarke 100
  Assagai Wall 100
  Asylum Wall 100
  Boadicea (E2) 101, 102
  Cracked Actor (E2 5b) 98, 99, 100
  Doubting Thomas (E5 6b) 98, 100
  Harijan (VS) 99
  Hoghton Quarry 98, 99, 100–2
  Hollow Earth (HVS) 99
  Jean Jeanie 99
  Mandarin (E2 5b) 98, 101–2
  Red Wall 100
  Rhododendron Arête (E3 6a) 102
  Trowbarrow Quarry 98–100
Land's End 45, 46
Le Chacal (E2 5c) 104
Lee, Dominic 62
leg wedging 99
Lennard, Paul 19
Lewis, P. 15
Lewis, Steve 49
Limbo (HVS 5b) 25, 26
limestone climbing 17, 80, 81, 105
Linney Head 11
Littlejohn, Pat
  in Devon and Cornwall viii, 36, 40,
    44, 45, 49
  in Southern England 62
  in Wales 1, 6, 10, 107
  in West Country 30
Little Orme 106, 108, 112
Livesey, A. 72
Livesey, Pete
  in Lake District 93, 97
  in Peak District 72
  in Wales 114
  in West Country 30
  in Yorkshire 80, 84
Lizard peninsula 45, 46, 48–9
  Amnesty (E2 5b) 45, 48

Bass Point 49
  Cull (E3 5b) 45, 48, 49
  Pen Olver (E4 5c) 49
Llanberis 109, 118, 119
Llandudno 108, 110, 111–13
  Detritus Wall 112
  Diamond 108, 112–13
  Gogarth 109, 110
  Marine Drive 110, 111
  Pen Trwyn 106, 108, 109, 110, 111
  Plumbline (E3 5c) 109, 111–12
  Specular Reflections 113
  Wall of the Evening Light (A2/E6
    6b) 109, 112, 113
Llangollen 103, 104
Lleyn peninsula viii, 109, 110
Llyn Padarn lake 118
Llyn Peris lake 118
Lockwood's Chimney, Doorpost v
Longleat Estates 32
Long Tall Sally (E1 5b) 67, 68
Long Wall (Chee Dale) 73
loose rocks
  Beachy Head 63
  Cheddar Gorge 31–2
Lost in Space (HVS 5a) 10, 12–13
Lower Sharpnose Point 36–40
  Fay (E4/5 6a) 36, 38
  Lunakhod (HVS 5a) 36, 38–9
  Mascon 38
  Middle Fin 38
  North Fin 38
  Out of the Blue (E2/3 5b) 36, 38
  Smile (E1) 38
  South Fin 37
  see also Culm coast
Lunakhod (HVS 5a) 36, 38–9
Lunatic (E4 5c) 93, 97
Lundy 40–4
  accommodation 41
  Black Crag 44
  Devil's Limekiln 43
  Devil's Slide 42, 43
  Diamond 43–4
  Exorcist (E3 5b) 40, 42–3, 44
  getting there 41
  Satan's Slip (E1 5a) 40, 42, 43, 44
  Smear? No Fear 43
  Watching the Ocean (E6 6b) 40, 44
  Widespread Ocean of Fear 44
Lynden, Mark 118

McFarlane, A. 6
McHaffie, Ray 89

Mad Dogs and Englishmen (E3 5c) 72,
  74
Main Wall (Avon Gorge) 28
Malham Cove ix, 80–3
Mandarin (E2 5b) 98, 101–2
Manic Mechanic (E5 6b) 103, 107, 108
Manikins of Horror (E3 5c) 103, 105,
  106
Marsden, Keith 36
Matheson, Rob 93
Max Buttress 74
Mayers, Steve 113
mental aspect of climbing 27
Mercury Connection (HVS) 47
Mercury (E2 5b) 45–6, 46–7
Mewslade Bay 5
Midnight Cowboy (E3 5c) 80, 81, 82
Millstone, Great Slab v
Mind Cathedral (E5/6 6a/b) 57, 58
Ministry of Defence, access agreements
  11–12
Mitchell, Paul 74–5
Mitre (E4 6a) 53
Moelwyns 113, 117, 118
Monks, Steve 6, 25, 49
Monster Crack (XS 5c) 62, 63–6
Moonchild (E4 5c) 93, 96–7
Moran, Jim 109
Morlais, Phobia 15
Morrison, M. 63
Mortlock's Arête (E4) 75–6
Mother of Pearl (E4 6b) 15, 17
Moulding, John 103, 107
Mountain Ash 15
Mount Sion East 10, 12
Moving Buttress 73

National Trust 32
Nemesis Wall 106, 107
Northumberland 85–8
  Angel Fingers (E1 5b) 85, 87, 88
  Bowden Doors 85, 87
  grading routes 86
  Greenford Road (E5 6b) 85, 87, 88
  Hepple 87
  Kyloe 85, 87
  Midgey Ha 87
  Sandy Crack (E2 5b) 85, 87–8
  Sandy Crag 85, 87–8
  Vertical Vice 87

Ocean Boulevard (E3 5b/c) 54, 56
Offa's Dyke Footpath 103, 104
Offspring (E5 6b) 67, 70–1

Ogmore 1–5
  Bigger Splash (E3 5b) 3, 5
  Bishop (HVS) 5
  Daughter of Regals 3
  Davy Jones' Locker 3, 4
  Exposure Explosion (HVS 5a) 1, 2
  Fire Wall 3, 4
  Hob Nob Bay 3
  Hunchback (E1) 4
  Martin Crocker routes 3
  Old Stable Tea Shop 2
  Phaser (E3 5c) 1, 4
  Pinnochio (HVS) 3
  Pluto (VS) 3
  Siren (VS) 5
  Sorcery Wall 3, 5
  Spellbinder (E4 6a) 1, 3, 4
  Tiger Bay 3, 4
  Warlock 3
  Wet Look Cave 2–3
Open Heart Surgery (HVS 5a) 60
O'Sullivan, P. 45
Out of the Blue (E2/3 5b) 36, 38
Oxley, Pete 7, 54, 57

Padarn Country Park 118, 119
Paradise Lost (E5 6b) 30, 34
Parker, Al 93
Parker, Dave 93
Parrock Quarry 94
Peak District
  Burbage Valley 67–71
  Chee Dale 72–6
  Wimberry 76–9
Pembrokeshire 10–14
  Bosherston Head 10, 14
  Castlemartin Artillery Range 10, 13
  Cauldron 11
  Deep Space 11
  Diedre (E2) 12
  Huntsman's Leap 11, 14
  Lost in Space (HVS 5a) 10, 12–13
  Lydstep 13
  Mother Carey's Kitchen 13
  Mount Sion East 10, 12
  Mowing Word 13
  Planet Waves (E2 5b) 10, 13
  Stackpole Head 10, 13
  Star Wars (E4 5c) 10, 14
  Swordfish (E3 5c) 10, 13–14
  White Tower 11
Penal Servitude (E5 6b) 89, 91–2
Pen Olver (E4 5c) 49
Penwith crags 46

Perihelion (HVS 5a) 59, 60
Perry Coma (E5/6) 60
Phaser (E3 5c) 1, 4
Phoenix 116, 117
Pillar Rock 93
Planet Waves (E2 5b) 10, 13
Plishko, Nick 76
Plumbline (E3 5c) 109, 111–12
Plum Buttress 73
Pollitt, Andy 103, 107, 109, 113
Pont Nedd Fechan 15
Portway (Avon) 25
Pretty, C. 45
Pull My Daisy (E2 5c) 118, 119–20, 122

Range West, south Pembrokeshire viii
Rasp (E2 5b) 67, 68–9
Raven Tor 72
Reecastle Crag 89, 90–3
Regan, Gabe 72
Rhoscolyn 108, 110, 111
Rhossili 5, 7
Ride the Wild Surf (E4 6a) 118, 120, 122
Robbins, Glen 52
Rouse, A. 59, 62
routes, grading 86

Sacré Coeur (E2 5c) 39
St Agnes Head 45, 46
sandstone climbing 88
Sandy Crack (E2 5b) 85, 87–8
Sandy Crag 85, 87–8
Satan's Slip (E1 5a) 40, 42, 43, 44
Scafell 93
Sea Walls (Avon) 25, 28
Sharp, Andy 1, 15
Shaw, Dave 114
Sheard, John 93
Shepherd's Crag 89
Shorn Cliff 19, 20–1
Silent Spring (E4 5c) 67, 70
Silvester, John 118
Sirplum (E1 5b) 72, 73
slate climbing 119, 120
Sloe Gin 73
Smith, Bob 85, 86
Smith, Haskett 114
Smith, Tommy 85
Snowdonia 109
Snowdrop Connection (E3 6a) 113, 116,
  117
Southerndown 1, 2
Space Buttress 10
Spain (E4 6a) 15, 18

Spellbinder (E4 6a) 1, 3, 4
Stackpole Head 10, 13
Star Wars (E4 5c) 10, 14
Stevenson, Alan 82
Stokes, Neil 76
Stoney Middleton 72
Strapcans, Arnis 19, 40, 43, 44
Sunset Buttress 32, 33–4
Sun, The (E3 5c) 109, 110–11
Survival of the Fastest (E4 6a) 103, 106, 107
Suspension Bridge Buttress 25, 26
Swanage 54–8
  Boulder Ruckle East 56
  Buccaneer (E2 5b) 54, 56–7
  Conger (E1 5c) 54, 57–8
  Fisherman's Ledge 57
  Freeborn Man 57, 58
  Lean Machine 56
  Mind Cathedral (E5/6 6a/b) 57, 58
  Ocean Boulevard (E3 5b/c) 54, 56
  The Ritz 57
Swindley, Gerald 103
Swordfish (E3 5c) 10, 13–14
Symonds Yat 20
Syrett, John 80

Tanygrisiau 113, 117
Tax Exile (E5 6a) 59, 61
Tennis Shoe viii
Ten Years After (E4 5c) 93, 94–5
Thomas, Dave 52, 53
Thomas, Phil 1
Thomas, Roy 6
Thriller (E4 6a) 7
Thurba Head 6–7
Tintagel, Il Duce viii
top-roping 85–6
Torquay 51–3
  Anstey's Cove 49, 53
  Berry Head 52
  Call to Arms (E4 5c) 49, 52–3
  Empire of the Sun (E6 6b) 49, 53
  Mitre (E4 6a) 53
  Sacrosanct 52
  Sanctuary Wall 49, 52, 53
Touch of Class (E2 5b) 104
Tour de France (E5/6) 27
Transformer (E3 6c) 6, 8, 9
Trowbarrow Quarry 98–100
tufa pillars 95
Turner, A. 49
Turner, K. 54
Two Tier Buttress 74

Upper Wall (Avon Gorge) 25, 28

Valleys (South Wales) 15–19
Verger (E2 5a) 39
Viggars, Dave 10

Wales 1–24
  Bank Holiday climbs 113–18
  Cader Idris 113, 114–16
  Clogwyn-yr-Eryr 113, 116–17
  Clwyd 103–8
  Craig-y-Clipiau 113, 117–18
  Dinas Rock 15, 17–19
  Dinorwic slate quarries 118–22
  Gower 5–10
  Holy Island 108, 110–11
  Llandudno 108, 110, 111–13
  Ogmore 1–5
  Pembrokeshire 10–14
  Southerndown 1, 2
  the Valleys 15–19
  Wye Valley 19–24
Wall of the Evening Light (A2/E6 6b) 109, 112, 113
Wall Street Crash (E6 6c) 71
Ward, D.G. 40
Ward, Matt 6, 19, 40
Warpath (E5 6a) 109, 110
Watching the Ocean (E6 6b) 40, 44
Watendlath 90–1
Watts, C. 63
West Country 25–35
West Route (Cheddar Gorge) 33
Whillance, Pete 89
Whillans, Don 67, 68, 69
White, Nick 40, 49
White Noise (E3 5c) 89, 91
Williams, Paul 109, 118, 121
Williams, S. 54
Wimberry 76–9
  Appointment with Fear 79
  Berlin Wall 79
  Blasphemy (E2 5c) 76, 79
  Blue Lights Crack 78
  Consolation Prize 79
  Freddie's Finale (HVS 5b) 76, 78
  Neptune's Tool 79
  Route One 78, 79
  Sick Bay Shuffle 79
  Trident 78
  Wristcutter's Lullaby (E6 6c) 76, 79
Winkworth, K. 54
Wintour's Leap 19, 20, 21–3
Wintringham, Ben 10

Wintringham, Marion 10
Witherslack Valley 95
Wombat (E2 5c) 80, 81–2
Woodcroft 19
Wristcutter's Lullaby (E6 6c) 76, 79
Wye Valley 19–24
  Ban-y-Gor 20
  Blitzkreig 22
  Burning Giraffe (HVS) 22, 24
  Dinosaur Heaven 22
  Eva Brawn 22
  Feline 22
  Great Central Cave 21
  Great Overhanging Wall (GO Wall)
    21–4
  Hyena Cage 22
  Isle of Dogs 22
  Jackal 22
  Kaiser Wall 22
  Kangaroo Wall (E2 6a) 19, 22, 23
  King Kong (HVS) 22, 23
  Laughing Cavaliers (HVS 5a) 19, 21
  Lurking Sear 22
  Never Say Goodbye 22
  No Musketeers Direct (E1 5c) 19, 21
  Pedestal 22
  Shorn Cliff 19, 20–1
  Symonds Yat 20
  Umbrella Girdle 22

Upper Terrace 22
Vulture Squadron (e4 5c) 19, 22, 23
Wintour's Leap 19, 20, 21–3
Woodcroft Quarry 21, 22
Wyndcliffe 20
Wyndcliffe 20

Yellow Edge (E3 5b/c) 25, 27, 28
Yellow Regeneration (E5 6b) 6, 8, 9
Yellow Wall (E3 5c) 5, 6, 7–9, 10
Yorkshire 80–4
  Bolt Revolt 82
  Cave Route (Right Hand) (E6 6a) 80,
    84
  Controversy (later Cry Freedom)
    82–3
  Cry Freedom 82–3
  Dominatrix 82
  Frankie Comes Too Soon (E5 6b) 80,
    82, 83
  Gordale Scar 84
  Kilnsey Crag 80, 82–3
  Limehill 80
  Malham Cove 80–3
  Midnight Cowboy (E3 5c) 80, 81, 82
  Slender Loris 80
  Terrace Wall 82
  Wombat (E2 5c) 80, 81–2
  Zero Option 83